PRAISE FOR DENISE ROY'S
My Monastery Is a Minivan

"Denise Roy takes you through her personal journey of balancing family, career, and spiritual practice. Her stories are humorous and heartwarming and will inspire you to cherish the blessings and wisdom that can be found in everyday life experiences. I highly recommend this book!"
—SUSAN STONE, author, *Memories in Moments*

"Warm, witty, and inspiring, Denise Roy's practical treasure-house of wisdom will open readers to God's 'sneaky' love hiding in the ordinary routines of life. The personal stories of the author and her family serve as a catalyst to lead us to the Boundless Love that is always already there even in the messes of daily living. It is a book that the whole family will enjoy reading, and it is a great conversation starter about family values and spirituality in the 'real' world. Guaranteed to bring tears, laughter, and comfort to your soul! Highly recommended for family life and adult education programs."
—BRIDGET MARY MEEHAN, author, *Praying with Women of the Bible*, president, The Federation of Christian Ministries

"As a priest and as a mother, I have so enjoyed reading Denise Roy's book. Her stories affirm our journeys, reminding us that all the ordinary and simple things of life are pregnant with wonder and possibility. They encourage and nourish us as parents who struggle to find time to pray and to meditate in the midst of ringing phones, soccer games, and standing in line for the restroom. She powerfully teaches us that in our being present to our daily lives and to life around us, we are present to and will encounter the holy and will discover that we are always standing on holy ground. Thank you, Denise, for the gift of this book."
—REV. DR. GAIL KEENEY-MULLIGAN, St. Aidan's Episcopal Church, Tulsa, Oklahoma

"This book reminded me how important the everyday moments we have with our children can be. The stories made me laugh, cry, and ultimately celebrate the greatest gift in my life—being a mother. Denise challenges the concept of wasted time; through her eyes the reader comes to understand that time spent noticing life, loving children, or nurturing family is time that builds memories and creates a space for one's soul to blossom."
—SHEILA ELLISON, author, *The Courage to Be a Single Mother*

"As we take up this book's unspoken invitation to become a fly on the wall of Denise Roy's home, the antics of our own family's life suddenly seem more delightful; we are no longer alone in the universe of invisible friends, dried-up french fries, and unraveled blankies. Her stories invite us to tell our stories; her wisdom, humor, and grace invite our wisdom, humor, and grace. Through the vulnerability of her words, Denise Roy becomes a guide for those of us who long for a practical faith with which to raise our families in this fast-paced culture."
—ROBERTA B. CORSON, PH.D., United Methodist minister and psychotherapist

"*My Monastery Is a Minivan* reminds us that moments of grace can come when we least expect them. Simple and profound, Denise Roy's spiritual memoir illuminates the challenges of family life with the glow of mindfulness. For a refreshing blend of insight and inspiration, read this beautiful book."
—DIANE DREHER, author, *The Tao of Inner Peace* and *Inner Gardening*

"If there is, indeed, a place where heaven and earth meet, it is in the pages of Denise Roy's book *My Monastery Is a Minivan*. Denise highlights the magic in seemingly ordinary events and reminds us to pay attention to the sacred lessons contained within them. Her stories call on us to be more aware, more human, and more compassionate as we move through the spiritual discipline called life."
—BETH WILSON SAAVEDRA, author, *Meditations for New Mothers* and *Creating Balance in Your Child's Life*

"Denise Roy's lovely book is a treasure chest of stories—lyric, ironic, moving, and deliciously funny stories—that remind the reader to look for God in the fabric of the everyday. *My Monastery Is a Minivan* creates a narrative window through which the holy ground of family life becomes visible."
—WENDY M. WRIGHT, professor of theology, Creighton University, author, *Sacred Dwelling: A Spirituality of Family Life*

"Denise Roy writes as one who truly sees, who knows the ruts, the potholes, and the high mountaintops that lead to all the holy places. Her vision is rare, precious, and deeply reassuring. Roy's exuberant, wistful, poignant, and outrageously funny stories dare us to wake up, to open the hidden doors in our own lives 'where the Divine peeks in and waves at us.' She invites us to embrace our lives—with the minivans, annoying phone calls, and poopy diapers—and discover the holy ground that exists right in our own backyard."
—REV. JANE ELLEN MAULDIN, D.MIN., author, *Glory Hallelujah! Now Please Pick Up Your Socks*

MY MONASTERY IS A MINIVAN

Lee,
Wishing you peace
and many blessings,
Denise Roy

MY MONASTERY IS A MINIVAN

Where the Daily Is Divine
and the Routine Becomes Prayer

---

35 STORIES FROM
A REAL LIFE

LOYOLAPRESS.
CHICAGO

LOYOLAPRESS.

3441 N. ASHLAND AVENUE
CHICAGO, ILLINOIS 60657

Cover design and image by Tracey Harris
Interior design by KTK Design

Library of Congress Cataloging-in-Publication Data
Roy, Denise, 1955–
My monastery is a minivan : where the daily is divine and the
routine becomes prayer /
Denise Roy.
p. cm.
ISBN 0-8294-1687-0
1. Christian life—Catholic authors. I. Title.

BX2350.3 R69 2001
248.4'82—dc21
                                        2001029489

Printed in the United States of America

01 02 03 04 05 PhoenH 10 9 8 7 6 5 4 3 2 1

To my children,
Ben, David, Matthew, and Julianna,
who teach me the joy
of present moments.

CONTENTS

ACKNOWLEDGMENTS

It goes without saying that, as a mother of four kids, I could not have written this book without the love and support of many people.

Thanks to those at Loyola Press who made this such an easy process: Jim Manney and Vinita Wright, for offering gentle guidance and encouragement; Rebecca Johnson, for steering me through the final stages; Heidi Hill, for copyediting; Terry Locke, Karen Kouf, Dan Connor, Trish Blake, and the rest of the staff, for giving great support. A special thanks to former editorial director LaVonne Neff, who gave me such an enthusiastic blessing early in my writing process, and to literary agent Joe Durepos, who generously offered his time and advice and encouragement.

My extended family sustains me with their love and wisdom, and I cannot imagine life without them. My sisters, Nancy Freschi and Teresa Souvignier, are my constant telephone and life companions, and I am deeply grateful to them and to their families—Mark, Christine, and Amelia; and Doug, Brian, Allen, and Hannah. I am thankful, too, for my brother and sister-in-law, Lisle and Paula Smith, and my nephews Brad and Garrett. My parents, Jeanne Cryan and Lisle Smith, gave us a strong foundation of love and faith, and that has made all the difference. My stepmother,

Lorraine Smith, always gives me words of encouragement. My East Coast family members—the many Roys of Maine and Florida—welcomed me with open arms and hearts. I am particularly thankful to Suzanne Roy, who edited some of my stories and offered her personal support as a fellow writer. Thanks also to my brother-in-law, Don Gerow, for his helpful feedback.

A special thank you to Mark and Nadine Priestley, Rita and Cliff Priestley, Caroline and Matt Wiley, Jack Colford and Margaret Lane, and all the other family members and friends who surround my three sons and bless their lives.

It is said that certain individuals are our soul mates; well, our entire family has found a soul mate in the Saso family. Patt and Steve Saso, and their children—Brian, Paul, and Mikhaila—have been incredible gifts in our lives. A special thanks to Patt, who gives me love and support and wisdom beyond measure.

If you are very lucky, you happen upon a community of faith that helps you to become more than you thought you were. Several years ago, we happened upon such a community, and our lives have never been the same. I am grateful to my many faith companions; I would name them all, but I'd run out of space. Thank you for taking us into your hearts and blessing us in so many ways.

Thanks also to Debbie Marsella, for her love and wisdom and deep friendship. Keep writing, Deb. Thank you to Christine Evans for gifting me with encouragement, inspiration, and a beautiful bowl for my altar. Sr. Barbara Williams is not only my children's adopted grandma, she is also a dear and wonderful friend. I also offer a special thanks to all the kindergarten moms who make me laugh every afternoon, and to Judy Yarborough and Sue Casellini, for being such great teachers.

Anyone who knows me knows my love of books. I would like to offer a word of gratitude to the authors who have been such an inspiration to me, especially Anne Lamott, Anna Quindlen, Thich Nhat Hanh, Rachel Naomi Remen, Lawrence Kushner, Annie Dillard, Frederick Buechner, Marcus Borg, and Deena Metzger. And thanks to Carolyn Foster, who teaches such inspirational writing classes, and to Arlene Goetze, who offers women a forum for their writing.

A big group hug to my children, Ben, David, Matt, and Julianna. They have come into this world with great gifts and loving hearts and have taught me more than I could ever have taught them. I am honored to be a part of their lives.

My husband, Paul, makes it possible for me to continue on my path. Without him, this book would not have been written. Period. Not only has he helped edit these stories; he has cooked, cleaned, taken care of kids, and given innumerable shoulder massages. His patience and good humor have been endless (and I promise that one of these days I'll get back to cooking!). He is my dance partner, my life partner, my soul partner, and his love sustains me every single day. *Je t'aime.*

INTRODUCTION

I used to think that a serious spiritual practice required one to leave the world behind and enter the ordered, silent, peaceful world of a monastery.

I used to think that God, or Spirit, or the sacred could only be found if certain conditions were met—like lots of time, lots of space, lots of quiet.

I used to think I knew something.

Now I know better. Now I'm a mother.

I spent four years studying theology at a seminary many years ago, but raising children has helped me to understand much more about spirituality and spiritual practice. It's one thing to read in a book about forgiveness or compassion and quite another to practice these on a daily basis. There is nothing like the whining of a toddler demanding the *blue* cup instead of the *green* cup, or the endless repetition of cleaning up toys and clothes and dishes, to develop your patience and perseverance. There is also nothing like the softness of your baby's cheek, or the hug of your child at bedtime, to convince you of the existence of God.

I'm sure that living in a monastery comes with its own set of graces and challenges. But I venture a guess that the holiest and wisest of monks would have a difficult time trading places with us, living in our homes with our kids and monthly bills and car-pool schedules. It's no wonder that most of us live much of our lives in a somewhat dazed, half-crazed state, one in which we are always in a hurry, thinking there's not enough time and *way* too much to do.

The stories in this book are about all of this.

I started out writing them just for myself. I discovered that as I paid attention to what was happening each day, even the simplest of moments held great wisdom. Putting the words down on paper helped me to see the meaning and mystery and magic that are already present in my everyday life. I began to appreciate that most of the moments of my life are wonderful moments—not stupendous, fireworks-in-the-sky-type moments, but clear, contented, I'm-happy-to-be-alive-type moments.

As I wrote, I also got more in touch with the realm of Spirit that is woven into our world and brings wisdom to our days. There is a love that surrounds and sustains us all, but we forget this. These are stories about trying to remember. They are stories about discovering that very simple things—like breathing and smiling and being really present—have the power to change our lives and our families and our world. They are stories of days that are full of worry and wonder, exhaustion and exhilaration, anger and awe. And they are stories about recognizing that our vocation includes working with the roots of violence and greed within ourselves so that these might be transformed, bit by bit, into compassion and peace and generosity of spirit.

It might be helpful for you to know a few things before you begin. Since I didn't write all of these stories at one time, my children's ages may vary in each. Today, my oldest son, Ben, is twenty; my son David is eighteen; my son Matthew is sixteen; and my daughter, Julianna, is five. They have been my greatest teachers, and as you'll see, they appear often in these pages. My husband, Paul, and I have been married almost twelve years, and he has been an incredible source of humor and wisdom and sanity in my life. He and I are both psychotherapists—a fact that, at times, drives our kids crazy. We all live in Silicon Valley in a house that we could never afford if we were buying it today.

As I was writing during this last year, I fantasized about sneaking off for a week or two to a beautiful beach house where I could work undisturbed. That, I'm sorry to say, remained a fantasy. Most of this book was written either in the middle of the night in my bathroom or in the middle of the day in our living room, where toys and soccer bags and an occasional kid surrounded me. But even this taught me a good lesson. There is no ideal atmosphere for writing *or* for spiritual practice. The present reality is perfect—even though it can be a bit exhausting and messy.

In the same way that I didn't write this book straight through from beginning to end, it's not meant to be read straight through. These stories can be picked up and read independently—during a child's nap, or while waiting for the kids to finish soccer practice, or when you're locked in the bathroom in order to get a moment to yourself. Perhaps you might gather with friends and read a story together and then share your own stories. We all need to be reminded that we are not alone.

My hope is that this book will help you to discover the wonder and mystery and wisdom that exist right now in your own life. If you think you don't have any stories, it means you haven't been paying enough attention to your life. Look carefully and deeply. They're right there, if you have the eyes to see and the ears to hear.

And so we embark on a journey—one in which we discover that nothing is off-limits as a potential source of wisdom, as the dwelling place for divinity. As monks and nuns of many traditions have been doing for centuries, we bring the entire world with us as we enter into our hearts, into our prayers, and into our monastery . . . which, in this day and age, just might happen to look a lot like a minivan.

1
Driving Lessons

Wherever you go, there you are.

Jon Kabat-Zinn

I've come to realize that it's often in the most unlikely of places that a sign appears, one that gives us just the message we need for our journey. Maybe it comes in the advice of a friend; perhaps it shows up in rays of sunlight breaking through dark clouds. If we pay attention, any moment or any place or any person might be the bearer of wisdom.

Years ago, I was zooming down the street, feeling pressured because I was late, hassled because of the traffic, and angry with myself for putting myself in that predicament. Yet another red light forced me to stop, this time right in front of a bakery. Exasperated, I had nothing to do but sit and look at the shop's front window. There I saw a hand-lettered sign that read, "Relax . . . You Have Plenty of Time."

How did that bakery owner know just what it was that I needed to hear? He or she had sent a message out into the universe, and it was now being received. The words had their intended effect, and I took a deep breath and smiled.

Frederick Buechner, in his book *The Eyes of the Heart,* invites us to see such messages as little signs that let us know we've turned up at the right place at the right time. He writes that "there is no telling where God may turn up next— around what sudden bend of the path if you happen to have your eyes and ears open, your wits about you, in what odd, small moments almost too foolish to tell."

> If we pay attention, any moment or any place or any person might be the bearer of wisdom.

3

We do not know where God might turn up next, or where our path will lead, but when we stop and ask for guidance, answers eventually come. These answers are not always as obvious as the signs that we see on the road, signs that tell us clearly to STOP or YIELD, that warn us of a DETOUR AHEAD, or that encourage us to PASS WITH CARE. But if we pay attention and look carefully for them and then heed their message, we discover that it is possible to experience transformation right in the midst of wherever we find ourselves. The very place we are now is the very place that holds all that we need for growth.

Cheese Lady

Many poets are not poets for the same reason that many religious men are not saints: they never succeed in being themselves. They never get around to being the particular poet or the particular monk they are intended to be by God. They never become the man or the artist who is called for by all the circumstances of their individual lives.

Thomas Merton

A funny thing happened on my way to Safeway. My daughter and I were returning home from her school when I remembered that we needed a few groceries. We drove down the road, the one on which the large Carmelite monastery takes up an entire city block, and the stoplight turned red. As we sat at the intersection, a car from the cross street turned left, passing my minivan. I made eye contact with the driver and her three passengers—Carmelite sisters out on a rare "outside" visit, probably keeping a medical or dental appointment.

And then I smiled. That could have been me.

From the time I was six until I was twenty-one, I had this sneaking suspicion that I was meant to be a nun. My guess is that it all went back to my first-grade teacher, Sister Regina Mary. You know, one of those early imprint things, like a newborn Canada goose that will bond with a mother goose or an airplane, depending on what it sees first. Six-year-old girls are very susceptible to such influence, and believe me, those early days of Catholic education were *all* about influence. I wanted to look like Sister, talk like her, be like her. It didn't matter that all I could see of her was about ten square inches of her face, with the rest of her encased in a full black habit.

We'll skip over all the years in which my favorite reading was Butler's *Lives of the Saints* (especially the story of the young mother-martyr who, shortly after giving birth, was led out into the coliseum to be eaten by lions, the milk dripping from her breasts . . . I kid you not, I remember reading this, although the name of the poor saint escapes me). Let's just say that my early conditioning was *very* powerful.

Then I ended up in college, worried that I was going to let God down in a *big* way if I didn't follow up on this vocation. I signed up for a religious studies course on Thomas Merton, the Trappist monk and prolific writer, and as a result I was convinced that not only was I to be a nun, I was to be a contemplative one at that. I wanted to go into seclusion, to live unfettered by the mundane world and be involved in holier pursuits, loftier ideals. (In fairness to Thomas Merton, he did not hold this position; he wrote that if you think you can run from the world, you can forget it, because you bring it all with you wherever you go.) But in my youthful zeal, I thought, *Why settle for the earth when the clouds are so much more mysterious?*

My convictions were strengthened whenever I'd go into Safeway and see women (most of them portly, dressed in muumuus, some with cranky kids in their carts) standing in the cheese aisle. They would be experiencing a major conundrum: Should they buy sharp or mild? Yellow or white? Swiss or Monterey Jack? One pound or two? *This* was my sign from God. I was *not* cut out to be a wife and mother. Move over Merton, here I come to the hermitage.

I actually signed up for a weekend retreat designed for young women who were considering religious life. I said good-bye to my boyfriend (who was more than a little befuddled by my departure, not sure if this meant our date was off for the Senior Ball). I arrived at the convent, and after about ten minutes of sitting in a room with forty middle-aged sisters, I had a terrible realization: I didn't want to spend the rest of my life living in a convent with only women. I left that weekend knowing that it was time to take Merton's advice and begin to pay attention to *my* heart, to who *I* was. Gradually I realized that my path was to be one of contemplation in the midst of the clutter and chaos of everyday life.

In my youthful zeal, I thought, *Why settle for the earth when the clouds are so much more mysterious?*

So, to fast-forward through the years, I married the boyfriend, had three sons, got divorced, remarried, had a daughter, and was now sitting at this intersection, smiling as my life passed before me—or at least beside me.

The light turned green and we continued our journey. I parked at Safeway, and my daughter and I ran in to buy—you guessed it—cheese. I chose a one-pound block of medium Cheddar. It was even on sale! I smiled at the woman beside me who had selected the Swiss.

To think I almost passed up this experience.

CarMa

Sometimes,
When it is all, finally,
Too much,
I climb into my car,
Roll the windows up,
And somewhere between backing out the
*   driveway*
And rounding the first corner
I let out a yell
That would topple Manhattan.
How do you pray?

Margaret L. Mitchell

I have been driving a minivan for eleven years. This fact makes me, according to the market researchers who study such things, "a dull mom driving a dull car."

Okay, maybe I do fit the profile: a middle-aged mom with kids, a mortgage, ten extra pounds, and no chance of getting smiles from guys in other cars.

But I get a little defensive when I see Internet chat rooms with topics such as "Minivans—When You Might as Well Be Dead." Mothers who still imagine themselves wearing motorcycle boots and listening to Jimi Hendrix write in to poke fun at those of us driving these wimpy mommymobiles. One mom wrote that driving a minivan "is like going around with a gigantic diaper bag tied to my ankle." Moms like this will only drive huge SUVs with smoked windows so they can put the kids in back and pretend they're still single and sexy. They don't fool me.

But I don't want to start another Mommy Wars. No matter what vehicle we drive—minivan, Urban Assault Luxury Vehicle, 1983 Suburu—let's face it: we're all spending more time schlepping kids around than we ever thought we would.

I just happen to drive an old Dodge Caravan with peeling blue paint and 110,000 miles. It has a lot of endearing qualities: a sliding door that rattles until you try to open it, and then it refuses to budge; French fries that are permanently wedged into the rear seat cushions; a rolling can of Diet Pepsi that keeps impersonating a broken transmission. My van is also a great storage unit. For instance, at this moment it contains the following: a plastic eyeball from Burger King, three weeks of school artwork, soccer socks that have stiffened beyond any hope of restoration, Magic Markers without caps, smashed Goldfish crackers, a broken cell phone that my mother insists I carry in case I break down on the freeway, a Halloween pin (it's now April), a squirt gun key chain, a pair of broken sunglasses, a packet of McDonald's ketchup, a tube of SPF-48 sunscreen, eight leaves, five receipts, four broken pencils, three French hens, two turtledoves, and an expired coupon for a car wash.

I always imagined I'd spend my days meditating, writing, maybe even changing the world in my spare time.

But then I grew up to drive a car pool.

So here's a math problem for you. If the driver of minivan A travels an average of ten thousand miles per year at an average speed of, say, thirty-five miles per hour and does this for eleven years, how many years of therapy will this driver need?

I read one woman's description of her vehicle as her "prison on wheels." Another mom speaks fondly of her $%#@van; she refuses to drive it on weekends. I know how they feel. It can seem endless out there on the road. Sometimes I get the feeling I'm going in circles.

Actually, I *am* going in circles. My usual car-pool route has a seven-mile circumference. Round and round and round I go, picking up children here, dropping them off there. It reminds me of a dog I had as a kid. Her name was Honey Bunch, and she looked like a miniature deer, with doe-like eyes and light brown hair. She was also clinically nuts. Apparently she had been weaned too young, which resulted in a variety of neurotic behaviors. The one I most identify with was her habit of circling the perimeter of our back-yard, hour after hour; as a result, her paws wore a deep rut in our lawn. There are days when I'm convinced that my tires have worn a rut in the road.

(I should note that Honey Bunch did have a variation in her routine: as she ran her laps, whenever she got to the spot just below our dining room, she'd take a giant leap up to peek in the window. This was great fun when guests came over for dinner. They'd be eating and conversing, and then every other minute they'd spot a brown flash out of the corner of their eyes. They'd look over, but see nothing. We'd time how long it took before they mentioned it.)

Sometimes I think my kids see me primarily as a chauffeur and that they might not even notice if another driver came and took my place. This thought occurred to me one Saturday afternoon. There was a torrential downpour, and while I would've preferred staying home by the fire, I had to get a package in the mail. So Paul drove me to the post office in the minivan, parked at the curb, and waited while I jumped out with the package. After mailing it, I fastened the hood of my jacket and braced myself for a run back to the van. I dashed down the steps, pulled open the van door, and bounced onto the seat. "Whew!" I exclaimed, shaking out my hair. "It's wet out there."

Imagine my surprise when I looked over and saw a man I did not know sitting in the driver's seat and staring at me. A puzzled seven-year-old boy stood behind his father, his mouth gaping as he peered around the headrest. I must have been a little in shock, because it took a while for it to sink in: I was in the wrong van.

"Uh . . . I'm sorry," I apologized. "I thought you were my husband and this was our van."

"That's okay," the man smiled. "I thought you were my wife. She's wearing a very similar jacket."

I smiled awkwardly and opened the door. "Sorry," I said again, getting out. I gave them a little wave after I closed the door. I saw our blue minivan parked a few feet away, and when I opened the correct door, Paul had a big smile on his face.

"What were you doing?" he asked. "I watched the whole thing in my rearview mirror. I thought I had lost you for good!" he teased.

This event sparked some disturbing questions: What if we chauffeur moms are interchangeable? What if we got behind the wheel of any old minivan, and nobody really noticed, or cared? As long as we drive the car pool and get everyone where they need to be on time, would there be any complaints? I DON'T KNOW!!! Do you?

After one too many laps around the car-pool track, I was craving a few days when I wouldn't have to drive anyone anywhere. A friend mentioned a silent meditation retreat that was being offered at a nearby monastery, so I traded car keys with my husband and went.

When I arrived at the retreat, I was shown to my own little monastic cell. It had a single bed, a small chair, a sink, a mirror, and a small closet. It was perfect. For three days I was served breakfast, lunch, and dinner. I had hours to pray and write and read. And I had nowhere to be, nowhere to go, nowhere to drive.

On the last day, I was sitting in the chapel, grateful for the silence and yet beginning to miss my family. As I sat there, I noticed that I was surrounded by beautiful stained-glass windows. And then the thought crept in: *My minivan has really stained glass windows.* Uh-oh, my mind was drifting. I brought myself back to the present moment, back to being transported by the angels to heavenly realms. And then I had another thought: *In my minivan, I transport the angels to heaven-knows-where. Stop it,* I told myself. *Get a grip.* Suddenly an onslaught of comparisons burst into my head: *In the monastery, I meditate. In my minivan, I mediate. In the monastery, psalms are sung. In my minivan, palms are flung. Repetitive schedules are found in both the monastery and the minivan: 8:00 A.M. chapel, 8:00 A.M. car pool; 3:00 P.M. chapel, 3:00 P.M. car pool; 6:00 P.M. chapel, 6:00 P.M. car pool.* The analogies continued against my better judgment. *Order pervades the monastery; odor permeates the minivan. One is filled with monks, one with punks . . .* I was starting to lose it.

I went back to my room to pack my things, and I picked up a book to put in my suitcase. Before I tucked it away, I sat in the chair to read one last chapter. Imagine my surprise when I came across this passage written by Zen teacher, poet, and father Gary Snyder:

> All of us are apprenticed with the same
> teacher—reality. . . . It is as hard to get the chil-
> dren herded into the car pool and down the
> road to the bus as it is to chant sutras in the
> Buddha-hall on a cold morning. One is not better
> than the other; each can be quite boring; and
> they both have the same virtuous quality of
> repetition. Repetition and its good results make
> the very activities of our life into the path.

And then I had a revelation. My monastery is not a silent
cell out in the wilderness. My monastery is a minivan. It is
also a kitchen, a child's bedroom, an office. My monastery
is in the heart of the world—in family life, with a child on
my lap, in my partner's arms.

It was time to go home.

The next day, as I was driving the car pool, I noticed a
bumper sticker that read: "I'd Rather Be Fishing."

Not me. The bumper sticker I'd pick for my minivan would
read: "I'd Rather Be Here Now." With the French fries and
the children and the rattling door. A minivan might not be
as good as a monastery for finding peace and quiet, but it is
precisely the place where I find the face of God.

I'm Not Nice Anymore

The greatest advantage of not having children must be that you can go on believing that you are a nice person. Once you have children, you realize how wars start.

Fay Weldon

It was one of those mornings in which if I held any notions of myself as a nice person, they were completely dispelled. I'm usually shocked at how full of rage I can get. One minute I'm smiling and patient and saying, "Come on, sweetie, you said you *wanted* to wear this dress," and the next I'm channeling something from *The Exorcist* and throwing the dress on the floor, yelling, "Fine, go to school naked!"

On this particular morning, I was running late. My alarm clock didn't go off, my curling iron broke, and my tolerance level for the Getting Dressed Debate was low. Julianna decided she wanted to wear just her tights with a shirt, skipping the dress. I tried the usual you-have-two-choices trick, which she rarely goes for anyway, and as the clock ticked, so did my anger meter.

Finally I blew. I pulled the dress on her, trying not to be too rough, but she cried anyway. Eventually we made it to the car, and I buckled her into her car seat. On the way to school I huffed and puffed and grumped and frumped; then I looked in the rearview mirror. My daughter had stopped crying and had fallen asleep. I realized, with not a little guilt, how tired she had been that morning. We arrived at her preschool, and I had to wake her up. I gave her an extra kiss and hug. Then I drove away feeling like the worst mother in the world.

Other moms have written about how hard it is to be a parent, and their words make me feel less alone and less afraid. Anne Lamott didn't realize until she had a child that she was a psychopath:

> When you think that you're somebody who is
> so peaceful and loving and giving that you will
> probably start dating the Dalai Lama soon,
> only it turns out that you're thinking about
> picking your child up by the ankles and spin-
> ning him over your head, or leaving him out on
> the front steps until he stops crying, it's very
> confusing.

Harriet Lerner, in her book *The Mother Dance*, conveys a similar message:

> Children will teach you about *yourself*. . . .
> They'll teach you that you are capable of deep
> compassion, and also that you are definitely not
> the nice, calm, competent, clear-thinking, highly

evolved person you fancied yourself to be
before you became a mother.

And the title of Linda Eyre's book—*I Didn't Plan to Be a
Witch: And Other Surprises of a Joyful Mother*—pretty
much speaks for itself. She describes how her image of
being the perfect mom disappears with a flash of fireworks
as she is replaced by the Wicked Witch.

I tried to remember these things on this particular morning,
but I couldn't shake the picture of my daughter's frightened
eyes looking at the person who is supposed to be her
anchor, the closest thing to God she knows. Driving away
from her preschool, I passed an orchard, and I pulled over

> I couldn't shake the picture of my daughter's frightened eyes looking at the person who is supposed to be her anchor, the closest thing to God she knows.

and parked. It is one of the last remaining
orchards here in Silicon Valley. This whole
area used to be known as the "Valley of
Heart's Delight" and was home to eight
million fruit and nut trees. Now silicon has
replaced the heart, and miles of concrete
and strip malls cover the most fertile soil
on earth. But this small acre of trees is a
reminder to me that life still bursts through
despite our attempts to bury it.

Somehow I knew that I had to sit in my minivan, look at
the apricot trees, and give myself time to heal. The sun was
brilliant, and the leaves remaining on the trees were glowing
green and yellow-gold. Gardeners had come through the
day before and had pruned the trees, leaving each one's cut
branches on the ground beneath it. I felt camaraderie with
these trees, for it seemed that that very morning I had been

pruned. I knew that the anger and the shortness of temper were not what my heart wanted to feel.

And so I sat. I recognized how tired my daughter was, how her little body is growing at such a fast rate, how she is seeking to be a separate person—an agenda much greater than my wanting to get to school on time. I recognized too how tired I was, how much I cared about image and schedule. I saw where I needed pruning, clipping, shaping—not in a harsh way, but in a gentle, guiding, gardening sort of way. I wanted to declare, "I'll never be so angry again," but I knew that was impossible. We all have our moments. We all get exhausted, reach our pressure point, and burst all over the ones we love.

I am not the perfect mom. She doesn't exist. Little children are great teachers of our limitations. Yet it is in those many moments when we fall from grace that we can begin to know ourselves. We cannot redeem everything. What we can do is respond with compassion toward our children and ourselves as we set out in search of wisdom again and again.

Ironing the *Gi*

One day, you'll make somebody a great wife.

Mariette Roy (Paul's mom) to Paul when he was fourteen

My husband is studying aikido. If you ask him why, he'll tell you it's because it's a wonderful way to integrate mind, body, and spirit. He'll say that because the graduate school where he teaches requires such discipline for all its students, he wants to really understand their experience from the inside. He'll describe the practice as a "Way of Peace" that helps him blend with clients' energy and thus makes him a better psychologist. Mostly, I believe him. But secretly, I think the fact that Steven Seagal is an aikido master has something to do with it. There is nothing Paul likes better than to watch Steven Seagal kick butt.

Now the proper apparel for aikido is a *gi*. This is a white shirt and pants set that is worn with a belt. The color of the belt lets others know what level you are at: white is beginner, black is expert, and various shades are in-between. Paul has always washed and ironed his *gi* every week, and I've never paid much attention. He's always ironing something.

But the other day, as I watched him carefully laying each pant leg on the ironing board and pressing it until perfect, I grew curious.

"How come you iron that thing if it's just going to get wrinkled?" I asked.

I know enough about aikido to know that within seconds of his initial bow, someone will throw him and he'll be on his back looking up at the ceiling.

"Because I want it to look nice," he answered, carefully placing the pants over a hanger.

"No, *really*." Excuse my incredulity, but I've never been strong in my ironing beliefs. I also knew that within ten minutes of the start of his class, the *gi* would be soaked with sweat.

"That *is* the reason. Now what I tell the other students when they gather around to ask why I keep it so nice-looking," he said with a wink, "is that if my *gi* is clean and pressed, they'll figure I'm a beginner and won't throw me."

"So they wonder why you iron it too?" I felt somewhat vindicated.

"Yup."

My curiosity remained. "Exactly how long does it stay unwrinkled?"

"Well, given that it's 100 percent cotton, I'd say that it's, uh, pretty well wrinkled before I reach the dojo."

Apparently, the students and I are not the only ones to question this ritual. When a fellow faculty member spied Paul proudly carrying his pressed and hung ensemble through the corridors of the school, he stopped to comment.

"Pretty clean," his colleague teased.

"Yeah, everybody gives me grief about it. Even my wife."

"So how do you respond to her?"

"Well, I tell her that since I'm already ironing my underwear, I may as well iron my *gi*," he joked.

> The more you practice, the dirtier your belt.

But we may be making headway. Paul came home yesterday and washed and ironed the *gi,* but not the belt.

"Guess what I heard today," he announced. "A student told me that you're not supposed to wash the belt. You see, in the old days, *everyone* had a white belt. And since most people don't wash things as much as I do, their belts would get darker the more they practiced. The notion of a black belt was that its wearer had been using it a long time, and thus was very experienced."

I'm not sure if this is an accurate fact or if this student was secretly sent by Paul's class to stifle his enthusiasm for dazzling duds, but I like this concept. It has the ring of truth, and it fits with my experience of stretch marks, sagging breasts, and gray hair: The more you practice, the dirtier your belt.

Teens

People ask me all the time how to be an effective parent. They reckon that since I'm still alive after having three teenage sons, I must know something that they don't. Or, since my husband and I are psychotherapists, they figure we must know The Magic Formula. Some people imagine that since we've taught parenting workshops, we must know how to phrase questions *just right* so that teens will give answers other than "Fine" or "What*ever.*" They fantasize that our kids pick up their socks, wear their pants around their waist, and have bedrooms without mold. They envision our children as perfect and us as perfect parents.

I hate to shatter such illusions.

Yesterday, after telling my son Matthew for the umpteenth time to get off the computer so that I could do my work and being told that what I was doing was not really work, I reached my limit. I needed to scream, so I went upstairs to my bedroom phone and called my friend Patt. She and her husband, Steve, are *real* parenting experts. They've even written a book: *10 Best Gifts for Your Teen.* It has great advice on how parents can navigate the turbulent teen years. Each of their ten gifts begins with the letter "R"— such as respect, responsibility, room, reconciliation. So I always call Patt when I need to vent.

"I HATE KIDS!" I shouted into her ear.

"I DO TOO!" she shouted back. (We've had this conversation before.)

She let me complain, and then she offered her unconditional support. *This* is why I call her.

"You have my total sympathy," she told me. "And let me tell you about last night." She proceeded to tell me that while she was making dinner, Brian (her fifteen-year-old) wouldn't stop kicking the TV cabinet door. It has one of those springs inside, and he kept opening it and letting it slam shut. "Brian, please stop it," she asked nicely. Of course he didn't. "Brian, please. Don't break the door." She had just fixed that door, and she was infuriated that he wouldn't stop. Then she started yelling, "STOP IT!" but Brian kept at it. "WOULD YOU STOP IT!" she screamed, at wit's end. Then he looked up at her defiantly, with a slight sparkle in his eye.

"Which of your ten Rs is going to make me stop?" he asked.

(It is amazing how kids know *exactly* which button to push in us.)

Patt was quick with a response.

"RAGE," she retorted. "REVENGE . . . RESENTMENT . . . RETALIATION . . . " She was on a roll and came up with a handy set of ten "shadow Rs." I thought these were brilliant. (But there's no truth to the rumor that she's using these as the basis for a new book called *The Dark Side of Parenting*!)

I'll let you in on a secret. Even parenting experts have trouble with their kids. I'm not sure I'd even call it trouble. Mostly, it's all part of the normal developmental process. The bottom line is that the job description for kids is to grow up and leave home. And the job description for parents, whether we like it or not, is to help them do so. In the process of learning to do this, all of us—children and adults—change and grow. We'll do much better if we relax and go along for the ride, acknowledging that this is a roller coaster with ups and downs and inherent conflict. We just need to raise our hands and shout, "Wheeeeeee!" We'll be fine.

After talking with Patt, I felt so inspired by her ten Rs (the light and the dark) that I thought I'd try my hand at a set myself. Parenting expert that I am, here are a few of my Rs. Come up with your own; you'll discover it's liberating!

RECITE

Over and over again, recite a simple mantra. Patt's favorite is *This is not about me. This is not about me.* Another favorite is *It's not my fault. It's not my fault.* Mantras such as these are particularly helpful at those times when you've asked a horrible question of your teen, such as "How was your day?" and are accused of prying.

R E U S E

If you happen across a winning formula that gets your kids
to talk, reuse it. For example, no matter how I tried, I
couldn't get seventeen-year-old David to give me anything
other than a grunt. Then I stumbled across a magic phrase.
As he strutted shirtless around the house,
glancing in every mirror he passed, I'd say,

> Mantras such as
> these are particularly
> helpful at those
> times when you've
> asked a horrible
> question of your
> teen, such as "How
> was your day?" and
> are accused of prying.

"Nice pecs." "Do you think so?" he'd ask
hopefully. Then we'd have a little talk
about how he was working out, and he'd
pick me up to show me how strong he
was. I thought he'd catch on when I started
every conversation this way, but he was
suckered in every time.

Now the opposite of reuse is also true. If it
doesn't work, drop it. You've probably heard that the defi-
nition of *insanity* is "doing the same thing over and over
and expecting different results." We forget this as parents.
We think that if we say just one more time, "Please clean up
your mess," then kids will do what we ask. Silly us.

R E M E M B E R

It's important in the heat of battle to remember that these
teenagers are the same souls who told you when they were
little that they were going to marry you, who brought you
crumpled dandelions and told you they'd never leave you. If
you look *really* hard at their eyelashes, or their cheeks,
you'll see the resemblance. If they don't let you get that
close during the day, sneak into their rooms while they're
sleeping. Just hope they don't wake up, or you're toast.

R U M B A
You and your kids are in a lifelong dance. You step close;
you step apart. Close. Apart. Apart. Apart. Close. You're
learning and they're learning, and you're going to step all
over one another's feet. Remember: No pain, no gain. Have
fun with it when you can, and when you can't, do what I
did: call a friend and scream.

R E B E L
Every once in a while, go on strike. Spike your hair and
see if anyone notices. Serve dessert before dinner. Dance
hip-hop to the kids' music. Give them some sense that
there's a secret side to you—it just might let them know
there's a real person in there.

R E I N C A R N A T E
This one is my favorite. In your next life, come back as
your kid's teenager. Enjoy every minute.

So there you have it. I bet you could come up with similar
sage advice. To be honest, parenting experts often don't
know what works. Which is okay, because parents don't
know either, and as they say, "Not knowing is the beginning of wisdom." We're all in this together. Those of us
who teach classes on the subject can swap stories with the
rest of you about what happens in our homes, and then we
can all weep and laugh together. Beyond that, we're not
much help. All those hours with your kids are yours. *You*
have to figure out what to do with them. But I know you
can do it. After all, you're better than a parenting expert—
you're a real parent.

Kitchen Wisdom

Rachel Naomi Remen chose the title *Kitchen Table Wisdom* for her first book because when she was growing up, people sat around their kitchen tables and told stories—and that was the way wisdom was passed along.

I know what she's talking about. I love my own kitchen table. We endeavor to eat dinner together at it almost every night, making heroic efforts to adjust our schedules in order to do so. At our table we experience spilled drinks, tipped chairs, sticky fingers, and sticky situations. We do grace before meals and some meals without much grace. We hold occasional family meetings around the table, and it is a place for homework and artwork and holiday feasts. Through all of these times, we tell stories, we laugh, we cry, and we pass wisdom along.

But I've realized that wisdom is not limited to the kitchen table. There are other places in the kitchen where it abounds.

KITCHEN FLOOR WISDOM

We have a priest friend with a mystical bent. He spends half of every week in solitude, in a quiet rustic cabin out in the middle of nowhere. He takes long walks every morning and finds all sorts of places to meditate. One of his most unique places was the hollowed-out trunk of a tree that had fallen long ago. Being an unconventional type, he decided to lie down in the tree trunk for his prayer. Of course, while lying there he had a beautiful vision and received great insight, which he then shared in the following Sunday's sermon.

I thought about his way of preparing for a sermon when I was asked to share some reflections for Mother's Day at our church. The day before I was to speak, I was still totally unprepared. It had been a crazy week, and I had had no time to myself. On that Saturday morning, we had two nieces over, and children were racing past me every two minutes. My teenage sons were blasting their music from radios and the computer, and the house was a disaster. The kitchen was a mess, and the floor was really, *really* dirty. One too many glasses of juice had spilled that day, causing that sticky sucking sound every time I lifted a foot. And when I stepped down, I'd hear a crunching sound—crushed Cheerios had started adhering to my shoes.

At the height of all this chaos, I was really desperate. Remembering our priest friend's experience in the tree trunk, I stood at the sink and yelled out to my husband, "Do you think if I lie down on this dirty kitchen floor, I'll have a vision?!"

(All of this did give me a new insight into why religious and priests are required to be celibate.)

At church the next morning, I began my reflections with my dirty kitchen floor experience. I went on to share my belief that it is right in the middle of the nitty-gritty tasks of nurturing, cleaning, feeding, and dealing with birth and death and all that comes in between that we receive everything we need in order to grow and develop spiritually. Our task is not to escape the dirty kitchen floor—though a quiet cabin *is* tempting—it's to daily practice being present to what's in front of us in the moment. That, to me, is the wisdom of the kitchen floor.

KITCHEN SHELF WISDOM

A client of mine is the one who taught me that if you really want to learn about wisdom, start with the kitchen shelf. She came into therapy with the goal of keeping her kitchen shelf clean and clear of any mess.

"Once I get it clean, I want it to stay that way!" she moaned. She hated the fact that her family members weren't cooperating, that the signs of daily life kept popping up over and over again—dirty spoons, spilled drinks, glasses left half full. She wanted order, and life was getting in her way.

"It's a good thing you haven't seen my kitchen shelf," I teased. As we talked (and laughed) about the whole situation, she realized that it's not the dirty kitchen shelf that is exhausting her, but her expectations. When she shifted her mind-set and began *expecting* that mess would gravitate to the kitchen shelf because that's what a shelf is for, she began to have a different experience. She began to feel a certain comfort in seeing the mess, cleaning up the mess, watching the mess gather again, and cleaning the mess. Instead of fighting the shelf, she began to practice Kitchen Shelf Meditation.

I could relate to what she was going through. I remember when my daughter was an infant, and I wanted nothing more than to keep the high-chair tray clean. On New Year's Eve, we had a group of friends over, and we shared our goals for the coming year.

"Finish the book I'm writing," said one.

"Start a small business with the money I've made on my stock options," said another.

It was my turn. "Keep the baby's high-chair tray clean," I mumbled. It was honestly the only goal my brain could come up with.

There's a part of me that believes that once I get the high-chair tray, or kitchen shelf, *really* clean, I have won and it'll stay that way. But reality is more like the "Baby Blues" cartoon in which the mom experiences that momentary exhilaration: "Let's see . . . the kitchen is clean, the laundry is done, and the baby is dressed . . . I guess there's only one thing left to do . . . " Then, in the next frame: "CRASH! SPLATT! WAAA!" And in the last frame, mom cringes and returns defeated: " . . . Start over."

Let's face it: the socks are going to keep showing up dirty, the dog hair is going to keep getting on the carpet, and dinner is going to need to be served tomorrow night and the next night and the next. We can fight these facts and let the repetitive nature of life turn us into raving maniacs. Or, we can find wisdom in the ordinary, the boring, the day-in-and-day-out routines.

I know, I know. That's the ideal. But that's what they do in monasteries. The wise ones say that repetition is a key discipline to learn if we are to make progress on this spiritual path of ours. Well, God knows *we've* got repetition! And we get even *more* practice, because the monks don't have children around.

Just listen to all the opportunities for growth we get, as described by writer Mary Roach:

> **Picking up after children is like shoveling during a blizzard. As you are dropping off the armload of stencils and kitty stickers on the arts-and-crafts caddy, doll clothes are accumulating, unbeknownst to you, on your bed. You are Sisyphus, eternally rolling the boulder uphill—and then looking around for a closet to stuff it in.**

I have choices to make when I look at these endlessly repeating messes. I can run screaming from the room, or I can see the hundreds of "present moments" that went into creating that clutter. If I look at it all and smile, I could come awfully close to enlightenment! If I adopt May Sarton's attitude and see putting clean sheets on a bed and making order out of disorder as sacraments, I might even experience a little of heaven here on earth.

Unfortunately, more often than not I'm griping, wanting to hurry through all the boring stuff so that I can get to what's truly important. The Mary and Martha in me have this endless debate, and it doesn't help matters that Jesus sided with Mary. I'd like to remind him that the only reason he *got* dinner was that someone thought serving meals was just a wee bit important.

Of course, we won't feel spiritually enlightened every time we clean the kitchen. But when we shift our expectations—when we see ourselves participating in the cyclic nature of the universe, and in family life, with all of the paraphernalia that comes with it—then we're experiencing the wisdom of the kitchen shelf.

KITCHEN SINK WISDOM

Standing at the kitchen sink, we can garner all kinds of wisdom. We have plenty of opportunities to practice mindfulness, doing dirty dish after dirty dish after dirty dish after dirty dish. We are so lucky.

Recently, I've begun practicing a new ritual at the kitchen sink. I adapted it from one that Rachel Naomi Remen describes in her other beautiful book *My Grandfather's Blessings*. She adapted it from a ritual a Tibetan nun taught her.

Each morning, I take a small empty bowl and fill it slowly to the brim with running water. Dr. Remen and I use our kitchen faucets; the original nuns probably used a clear mountain stream. For the bowl, I use a white marble bowl that was part of a mortar and pestle set. It is heavy and cool and rests solidly in my palms as I do my meditation.

I turn the water on and let it run. And then I do a reflection, similar to the one described by Dr. Remen:

> As the bowl fills, you reflect on the particulars
> of your life, whatever they are. The people with
> whom you share your time, your state of
> health, whatever problems you face, what skills
> and strengths you have, your disappointments
> and successes, your worries, your personal gifts,
> your personal limitations, your home, all your
> possessions, your losses, your history as a
> human being. As the bowl fills, you receive
> your life openheartedly and unconditionally as
> your portion.

I fill the bowl to the brim; when it is full, I set it on the windowsill over my kitchen sink. Some people put it on a personal altar or on some other special place. I find that just over the kitchen sink is an excellent place; I constantly see it and am reminded of everything that life has given me.

At the end of the day, I empty the bowl and turn it upside down on the shelf until the next morning. This is a process of letting go, of waiting until the morning light to once again receive all that life holds. It reminds me of something I did as a child. The first thing each day, I would recite the Morning Offering, a prayer dedicating all that I did that day to God. Then, at bedtime, I would give thanks for all that had gone on during the day.

Rituals and prayers such as these are very helpful in our modern lives. I was reminded of this when I heard a radio interview with a Tibetan monk who is now living in this country. He spoke about how life in Tibet is completely organized around spirituality—from the moment you wake up until the moment you go to sleep, you continually experience, through various practices, your deepest self and your connection to all that is. Here in the United States, however, he sees that life is very different.

"It is very hard to live in a society that is organized around shopping," the monk said softly. He is a very wise monk.

The kitchen sink is as good a place as any to begin a daily practice. Given that we spend more time there than we do many other places in our home, it can be a powerful space to practice mindfulness and receptivity. There, we can begin to embrace the whole—all that is clean as well as all that is dirty; all the joys as well as all the sufferings—experiencing the wisdom of the kitchen sink and the development of a grateful heart.

The Little Way

At any given moment, we might, if we become fully present, feel the pull within us—that gravity of grace drawing us home to our deepest selves. Perhaps we find ourselves setting out on a journey, and we're not sure why. We embark on a pilgrimage, compelled to go, longing to remember that which feels like a fragment of a dream, a whisper of something important that could disappear if we don't follow where it leads.

My morning started out like many others—I sipped my coffee and glanced through the newspaper. Turning the page, I saw a large picture of St. Thérèse the Little Flower. Curious, I read the article. It gave a short biography of this young saint: She died in 1897, when she was only twenty-four years old, and she would likely have remained unknown had she not written her autobiography at the request of her sister. *Story of a Soul* was published after her death, and thousands have since identified with the "Little Way" of love that she professed. The article went on to mention that her relics were on a world tour and would be at the nearby Carmelite monastery that day.

Perhaps this caught my attention because Thérèse was my confirmation saint, and I had added her name to my own when I received that sacrament at age thirteen. Perhaps it was because she had recently been named a Doctor of the Church, one of only three women ever to receive that title. Perhaps it was because this was an opportunity to go once again to visit the beautifully silent Carmelite monastery. For whatever reason, when I turned the page, I could not let go of the feeling that this was where I was to spend my morning.

After I dropped the kids off at school, I was going to run a few errands, but I once again felt a mysterious pull and turned my minivan in the direction of the monastery. I justified this detour by telling myself that on this Monday morning there would be very few people at the monastery and I could just run in for a quick peek—a peek at what, I wasn't even sure.

When I arrived, I was surprised to discover that there was no parking. For blocks around this quiet residential neighborhood, cars filled the streets. Firefighters and police officers and men in suits directed traffic. Eventually I found a spot and began my walk toward the chapel, joining my fellow travelers.

As I stepped through the wrought-iron gate, I felt a shift, a change in my normal space-time continuum. It was as if I was stepping into an ocean of holiness; it surrounded me, and with each step I felt more deeply immersed in it. The place itself held some of this holiness: It was in the Carmelite chapel, with decades of chants and prayers embedded into the very walls and marble pillars; it was in the shady grounds, with its abundance of olive trees and rosebushes and rich brown earth; it was in the butterflies and the hummingbirds, in the spiders weaving webs among the thorns, and in the birdsong that filled the air. The saint's relics and her memory held some of the holiness. She was the catalyst for this great gathering of ordinary people; she was there to simply remind us that in this universe of ours, love is the only thing that works.

But most of the holiness resided in the people who had come to pay homage to Thérèse. It was in the schoolchildren dressed in uniforms, whose behaviors alternated between serious attention and exuberant laughter as they gloried in the sunlit day. It was in the elderly men and women who made their way slowly up the stairs, living reminders of those who make the effort, day in and day out, to grow their hearts. It was in the men in their dark suits who guarded the gates, their seriousness betrayed by the tiny rosebuds pinned on their lapels, giving us a glimpse into their longing for beauty and love. It was in the people who brought soda bottles filled with water, hoping just to touch the plastic covering that enveloped the saint's elaborate tabernacle so that the water might be blessed and they might bring home a little of this ocean of holiness. It was in the mothers and fathers who held their children, who carried their toddlers up to the altar of roses, who whispered the story of one soul into the little ones' ears in the hopes that they would discover the story of their own souls. It was in the cloistered sisters of this little saint, the women who sat hidden behind the grating in the sanctuary of the chapel, whose constant prayers hold up the sky.

I sat in the chapel and watched the people arrive in waves, catching my breath because so much goodness and faith was hard to take in. Then, in the midst of all this holiness, one woman caught my attention. She had managed to push a large stroller with an infant in front and a two-year-old in the rear up the stairs and into the chapel. She blessed herself with holy water and then moved in the line down the center aisle, waiting her turn to approach the relics of Thérèse. When she arrived at the casing, she bent down and lifted her two-year-old out of the stroller so that he could have a better look. After a moment she proceeded to the altar, smiling at her young son's delight in the roses that adorned a photo of the saint. They whispered together for several minutes, then the woman made the sign of the cross, genuflected, put the boy back in the stroller, and went out the side door.

It was time for me to leave as well, and I went outside. I saw the woman approaching, and something inside me urged me to go up to her and introduce myself. I asked her a simple question: "Why did you come?" It was a question that I had been asking myself; in asking her, I thought I might find my own answer. She graciously responded.

"Oh . . . because it's Thérèse . . . Thérèse taught her 'Little Way'—that what is important to do is simply the ordinary things of life, but to do them with extraordinary love. Her prayer showed her that even the smallest action, done with love, is more important than great deeds done with no love. In my life right now, I'm home with my kids; I don't do anything great. But she gives me hope that even I might live a life that makes God smile."

I asked her how many children she had, and she paused. "Four," she answered. "I have a daughter that's six, and these two boys. But my oldest son died two years ago. He was seven. He had leukemia."

Sometimes we are more than we think we are. I believe there are some grace-filled people; we call them saints, or gurus, or great teachers. They carry with them a transformative power, and when we get close to them, we feel changed. Yet I also believe that this same grace lies hidden in us all, and we are blind to it much of the time.

All over the world, pilgrims arrive at sacred sites by the busload, traveling in search of *something*. We get to the site, and we see the object of all our projections of holiness: the Bodhi Tree, the silver star in the belly of a cave, a sliver of wood, a jar of tears. We begin to scratch our head and ask again, "What was it I was seeking?" We look around, and we begin to notice who else has come. So here we are, all together; we've all shown up, we've all received our message to be here at this appointed time. What does it mean? Who has called us, and what is it that we are to see?

What if . . . What if all of the sacred objects are a divine ruse, a playful pretext to get all of us to show up together so that we might look at *one another* and remind one another of who we really are? What if we discover that the holy ground is inside of us, so that with Jacob we proclaim, "Surely God is in this place, and I did not know it"? What if we come to see that enlightenment, or sainthood, is not a permanent state but comes only in moments, moments in which we choose to love deeply and well?

Thérèse was once a little girl who held her father's hand on the way to church, eager for the pastries he bought her after Mass. She carried the unfulfilled vocations of her mother and father and from an early age aspired to be a nun and a saint. As a young woman she longed to be an apostle, a missionary, and most of all, a priest, carrying the message of love to the corners of the earth. And here she was, paradoxically getting her wish, traveling the world proclaiming her gospel of love from beyond the grave.

As I left the monastery, I watched the tabernacle of her relics being carefully placed into a van, and a few moments later, the remains of the little saint were driven off to the freeway. Were commuters aware that a saint was passing by? Or do saints pass us all the time, and we do not know it?

The real pilgrimage is one we can make every day as we go to the center of our lives, look around, and see who is there with us. They've all arrived: our children, our fellow workers, our partners, our parents, our community. These are our fellow travelers, the ones who have shown up in this time and place. Holy ground exists right in our own backyard when we love in ways we didn't think we could, when we call upon our best selves to be present to one another. We make a journey to love, right in the midst of all of our diapering, cleaning, feeding, grieving, laughing, holding, living, dying—doing ordinary things with great love.

II
Breathing Lessons

Breathing in, I know that I am breathing in.
Breathing out, I know that I am breathing out.

Thich Nhat Hanh

I do not know why certain memories follow us through the years while others seem to vanish almost as quickly as they form. And it surprises me how it is often not the big moment that clings to our soul, but the little one that is barely discernible to any other eye.

I have one such memory. It happened many, many years ago, at dawn. I was four years old.

It is still dark, although I sense that morning is coming. I hear someone in the other room, and so I climb out of bed and creep down the hallway toward the light. Through sleepy eyes I see my mother in the dining room, ironing clothes by the light of a lamp. On the table there is a large laundry basket filled with my father's shirts and my play outfits. My mother smiles, surprised to see me awake at such an early hour. She pulls up a chair for me to sit on, and I watch as she sprinkles the clothes with the water from a glass soda bottle that is fitted with a plastic nozzle. After we talk awhile, she sets down the iron and looks at me. "Since you're such a big girl now, would you like a cup of coffee?" Incredulous that I am being given this symbol of adulthood, I nod eagerly. She pours me a cup that has more sugar and milk than coffee in it, and as I sip, I am warmed by a deep sense of connection.

It is humbling, as a parent, to realize what it is that children remember. All of our many efforts to provide them with fancy gifts or exciting trips may not, in the end, matter as much as the feeling they get when they sit in a tree or on our lap. For all of us, the memories that contain the greatest joys are usually of times when we felt connected—to ourselves, to nature, to our parents, to God. Even though these moments happened many years ago, we continue to carry within us something of their holiness.

It is so easy to not experience such connection. Our busy lives pull us away from ourselves, so much so that we even forget how to breathe. We rarely hold still. Our bodies might be sitting with our children, but our minds are racing off in many other directions. When our little ones look us in the eyes, they know we are not there.

> For all of us, the memories that contain the greatest joys are usually of times when we felt connected—to ourselves, to nature, to our parents, to God.

And while it is not easy, it is vital that we resist this way of life that pulls us away from ourselves. For we teach our children not so much by preaching lessons or dogma to them as by the way we walk and sit and see the world. They will learn to breathe and smile and be compassionate and connected to themselves and to their world through our example.

My early memory of my mother's presence to me reveals the enormous power in the simplest of human interactions. A simple touch, a gesture, a deep seeing of another—these are the ways grace comes into our world. It is rare that grace comes through burning bushes or parting seas; we have to look a bit harder to see its presence at work in our lives. But it's there.

I had a dream recently that, like my early memory, also had a laundry basket in it. In the dream, people were standing around looking up at the sun, waiting for it to come down from the sky. They were growing impatient because it wasn't coming. Then I noticed that small white flakes were falling all around us. I grabbed a laundry basket and began catching these flakes. As I did, I felt deep joy.

Then the scene switched to a small group that was discussing what had just happened. It became clear to me that everyone seemed to be looking for the big experiences of spiritual ecstasy, and they were inevitably disappointed. I told the group that we just needed to take our laundry baskets and catch all of the wonderful moments that were falling down all around us. I told them that what we're looking for exists in the falling flakes, not in the big sun. Then I woke up.

Perhaps our deepest feelings of joy and connection lie as close as our next breath, our next hug, our next cup of coffee in the early dawn.

Sitting in Happy

A serene mother rocks the universe in her arms and all is well.

Vimala McClure

If you were to visit my house, it's likely I would offer you a seat in Happy. And you'd probably agree with me—it *is* a wonderful place to sit.

Happy is the name of the half-leather, half-vinyl, dark blue rocker-recliner in our family room. It was my favorite place to nurse my daughter, Julianna, when she was a baby. Those moments were wonderful. I had no choice but to slow down, breathe, and relax enough so that the letdown reflex would work. She would nurse for a few seconds, peeking at me out of the corner of her eye, excited that she finally had my full attention. But she'd smile so much that she'd release the suction. Various games would then begin, including "Make a Face," "Smell My Feet," and "Bonk Mom's Head." There are few experiences in life that equal that little mutual love-in.

When Julianna was just a little more than a year old, she somehow intuited the meaning of the word *happy*, knowing that it had a lot to do with whatever was happening in that chair. So one day, instead of making the little clicking sound she usually made whenever she wanted to nurse, she looked up at me, pointed to the chair, and said, "Happy." That was the christening of the chair, and we have called it by that name ever since.

I no longer have a little one tugging at my leg, begging me to "sit in Happy." When I did, it was easier for me to remember to stop and sit, to come back to the present moment and simply breathe. But there are times when I still hear a little voice, this one from inside myself, pulling at my heart and asking me to sit in Happy.

When I listen to the voice and make the choice to pause in my rapid journey through space and time, I find home again. In that place, I remember who I am. I connect with my body by slowing down my breathing. In that moment, there is nothing else to do, nowhere else to go. Very often, I practice the simple breathing meditation described by Buddhist monk Thich Nhat Hanh:

> **Breathing in, I calm my body.**
> **Breathing out, I smile.**
> **Dwelling in the present moment,**
> **I know this is a wonderful moment!**

No matter what is happening, I can smile. I can know that this is a wonderful moment. There is no desiring of anything; it is a place of quiet joy.

Thousands of years ago, the psalmist put into words the feeling of sitting in Happy:

> Lord, my heart is not proud;
>   nor are my eyes haughty.
> I do not busy myself with great matters,
>   with things too sublime for me.
> Rather, I have stilled my soul,
>   hushed it like a weaned child.
> Like a weaned child on its mother's lap,
>   so is my soul within me.
>
> Psalm 131

When I sit in Happy and become centered, my children are drawn into this place as well. One day, Julianna and I were sitting quietly together in the chair. Then David, my eighteen-year-old son, ran over and draped his six-foot-one-inch body across us both. He was leaving for college the next week; as he sat on my lap, he gave me a hug, pretending he was still my little boy. We knew that life would soon be very different, and we all smiled in our awareness of that moment as a wonderful moment. Then his girlfriend knocked at the door, and he jumped up; the moment moved on, yet it stays in my heart.

Any chair, at any moment, can be Happy. Whenever we choose to sit in Happy, we come back to center again. We align ourselves with the love that patiently waits for us to slow down, pause, and invite it in. When we still and quiet our souls within us, we discover that we've never been separate from God or from one another. We experience the connection to all that is.

Doors

Entrances to holiness are everywhere.
The possibility of ascent is all the time.
Even at unlikely times and through
unlikely places.

Bamidbar Rabba 12:4

Julianna's favorite art projects these days always involve tape. She peels the stickers off of apples and bananas, then attaches these in designs all over the kitchen walls. She measures her height with string, then tapes the string to the side of our bookshelf. And she labels everything, everywhere. She carefully writes out the names of items on pieces of paper, then tapes these to each one so we'll all know what they are: FLOWER VASE, VCR, PIANO. Last week, after hearing me yell (quite frequently) at her six-foot-tall brothers to stop wrestling, she sat down and wrote out the word *NO* fourteen times. Then she cut out each one and, with tape in hand, fastened the command to walls everywhere. There is a NO near the oven, a NO near the stereo, a NO on the pantry door. I'm thinking of just taping one to my forehead.

This week she has a new project. She has drawn tiny, colorful doors, about four inches tall by two inches wide, and has attached them to various walls, each door held in place with forty-nine pieces of tape. A little orange door in the entry hall was the first to catch my attention. Then, while putting away a pencil in the desk drawer, I was surprised by a tiny pink door just above the Post-it Notes. I even found a door in the laundry room.

Every now and then, I see Julianna standing before one of these miniature doors, talking quietly, apparently welcoming whoever has just come through. Sometimes, she tells me, it is one of the mice who live in our castle; often it is one of her invisible friends.

I find myself breaking into a smile whenever I pass one of these little doors. Maybe it's because I'm Irish, and my Celtic heritage, with its belief in "thin places," is seeping into my imagination—or perhaps into my home. "Thin places" are those places where the everyday world and the realm of the divine meet, where the walls that we normally experience as solid, dividing one reality from the other, are permeable. They are the places—or even the moments—where God leaks through, where the divine peeks in and waves at us. In these holy places, extraordinary things happen.

Maybe doors are all over the place, and grown-ups are blind to them.

As I pass these doors, I wonder: maybe my daughter knows something that I've forgotten. Maybe doors are all over the place, and grown-ups are blind to them. Maybe this is what Jesus was talking about when he said the reign of God is spread out all over the earth, and people just don't see it. And maybe that's why we need to become like children—in order to have eyes that can find the doors, the crevices, the cracks, the thin places in our everyday ordinary lives where we might catch a glimpse of the divine.

Three Moments of Grace

The sacred moments, the moments of miracle,
are often the everyday moments.

Frederick Buechner

I.

My father and I sit on opposite sides of the political fence. Usually I just try to avoid discussions about politics whenever we're together, but during this last year he began sending out massive e-mails to his children in an attempt to show us the error of our ways. It got so bad that every time I saw his name attached to an e-mail, I'd sigh and delete it before even reading it.

This morning, when I sat down to write these reflections on grace, I wasn't sure how to begin. So I sat and meditated. It didn't help. Then I thought I'd distract myself and check my e-mails. Sure enough, there was another one from my father. *Oh, brother, here he goes again,* I thought. My finger was on the delete button when something told me to open the e-mail. It was one of those stories making the rounds in cyberspace. I read it and smiled. Grace even arrives by e-mail.

The man whispered, "God, speak to me," and a meadowlark sang.

But the man did not hear.

So the man yelled "God, speak to me!" And the thunder rolled across the sky.

But the man did not listen.

The man looked around and said, "God, let me see you." And a star shined brightly.

But the man did not notice.

And the man shouted, "God, show me a miracle!" And a life was born.

But the man did not know.

So the man cried out in despair, "Touch me, God, and let me know you are here!"

But the man brushed away the butterfly and walked on.

Don't miss out on a blessing because it isn't packaged the way that you expect.

I I .

Last week, God waved at me. It was a little unsettling, I must admit. I was trying to not notice, to look preoccupied with the book I was reading—Kathleen Norris's *Amazing Grace*. Sometimes it's easier to read *about* amazing grace than to recognize it at work in our everyday lives.

I was minding my own business, sitting in the nice quiet reading area of our public library. I had selected my seat carefully—one of eight comfortably cushioned chairs, all empty, facing a huge stone fireplace. The library was fairly deserted, and I figured that if anyone else did come to sit in *my* area, he or she would keep an appropriate distance.

Wrong. After ten peaceful minutes, I heard a commotion coming toward me—a walking crowd of noise. I looked up to see five people approaching me—three adults who were developmentally disabled and two young women escorting them. Of course, they surrounded me, selecting the nice cushiony chairs immediately next to me.

The man touching my right elbow was in his early twenties. With immense delight he tore pages out of the free magazines he had picked up in the library's lobby. As he ripped each page out, he talked nonstop about all the exciting things he was finding.

Determined to look undisturbed, as if I hadn't even noticed anything unusual, I kept my eyes on my book. The man touching my left elbow didn't say a word. He just looked down at his lap.

Then I began to hear giggles. It was actually a sort of whooping sound mixed with laughter, and out of the corner of my eye I detected an arm moving wildly. I peeked. Across from me sat a woman in her thirties, her head shaved, laughing and whooping and waving—at me.

I smiled and gave a little wave back. She increased the size of her wave, delighted by my response. One of the caregivers looked apologetic. She signed to the woman, who I now realized was deaf, and then whispered to me, "Sorry to disturb you."

"No problem," I said, smiling. I attempted to return to my reading.

Then the magazine tearer started handing me pages. He could hardly contain his excitement and wanted to share some of it with me. I took the pages one by one, smiling and thanking him. Then the giggles started up again. I looked over to see the waving woman trying to get the attention of a proper-looking gentleman who was browsing at the magazine stacks. She kept up her waves, but he did not respond. He refused to avert his eyes from the magazine he was reading. Finally she gave up. She sighed, then curled up in her chair and fell asleep.

And that's when grace began to have its effect on me. In the presence of these joy-filled people, I had this funny feeling that I should go and sit at their feet and learn from them. What do they know that I don't? They're so free to laugh, to smile, to wave. In comparison to them, I felt stilted, boxed in by my own self-consciousness, guessing that I had more in common with the somber man at the magazine rack. I remembered something that author Rachel Naomi Remen wrote: "The way in which we go to the grocery store may tell us everything about the way in which we live a life." *How many times a day,* I wondered, *am I blind to grace? How many times do I refuse an invitation to joy?*

Eventually the magazine tearer finished with his pile of magazines and sat quietly. All noise subsided. Since my area of the library was once again "under control," I somewhat reluctantly went back to my reading.

The book on my lap was opened to an essay entitled "Grace." Ironically, it was about a baby in an airport who was waving with absolute delight at the people walking by. "Our drab departure gate," Norris writes, "had become the gate of heaven." The message was that God finds a way to let us know that *in this place,* wherever we are, God is with us.

I almost whooped.

III.

When I was pursuing my Master of Divinity, one requirement I needed to fulfill was "Field Education," which meant working with people in settings beyond the school walls. I was scheduled to direct retreats at a local retreat center, alongside a number of male seminarians. I was also six months pregnant with my first child.

On the first evening, three retreatants were assigned to each director. One of the people assigned to me was a nun in her late sixties. She smiled tensely as she came over to meet me and to schedule our first session; we set a time for the next morning.

When she came in the next day, she entered quietly, but that changed shortly after she sat down. She was furious. The room she had been given was dirty and had no view. And she had been assigned *me* as her director. I was neither a religious nor a man, and this infuriated her. "These things should've been spelled out in the brochure the retreat center sent out," she bellowed. She had even gone to the coordinator of the center to request a different director, but he had suggested that she work with me, that perhaps God was at work in the pairing of her with me. He reminded her that on her application, under the section where it asked, "What do you most hope for from this retreat?" she had written one word: "Surprises."

She was not pleased.

After her initial tirade, she spent the rest of the session in tears. She had struggled with depression and guilt and workaholism all her life, and now, in her later years, she felt utterly and completely alone. For decades she had been having dreams of being pregnant, and she didn't understand what these meant.

For five days, I listened to her, made suggestions for her prayer, witnessed her desire to give birth to herself. She gave up trying to change directors, but on the third day she finally got her room changed to one with a view. Then croaking frogs outside her window kept her awake all night long. She kept getting her surprises.

Slowly, as each day went by, she shared her story. For the first time she talked about a long-held secret, about committing what she thought was an unforgivable sin. And she remembered that when her mother was dying, her mother had told her that she had never wanted children. Perhaps, she now realized, that is why she was never held.

Gradually during the retreat, this woman gave birth to herself. On one of the last days she shared with me a dream from the previous night; this was not a dream of being pregnant, but one of holding a child. Her anger at me, at my belly, at sexuality, at dirty rooms was now dissipated. At our final meeting, she came in and sat down. "On these retreats, I always want the best director, one who is well known," she told me. "I was angry that you were the one assigned to journey with me through these days. Now I realize you *are* the best, because you're the one God gave me." She gave me a hug good-bye. "Thank you," she said.

"Thank *you*," I responded, feeling both humbled and awed by the movement of grace.

Teenie Beanie Babies

If I had had a chance to read the newspaper that morning, I would not have been standing in line at McDonald's on what turned out to be its craziest day of the year.

I figured it was just a busy Friday. I had promised my then two-year-old daughter some French fries, and so I dutifully stood in a line of about five people. Of course, Murphy's Law kicked in, and it became the slowest of all the lines, with everyone else in the place passing us by. But I decided there was no rush. I smiled at the woman in front of me and resigned myself to the inevitable. And then I noticed something peculiar. Everyone was walking out with Happy Meals. *Everyone!* Not just the folks with kids, but old women, young women, and even a few men. The woman in front of me sighed and turned around.

"Did you see the front page?" she asked. I shook my head.

"Beanie Babies," she moaned.

As she said this, I realized that there were now forty-six people behind me, envious of my place in line.

That's when a couple of things happened. First, I began to think about how nuts people are, that they would endure an hour-long wait for a toy that was not worth more than

$1.49. Second, I changed my order. I decided to get a
Happy Meal along with my daughter's so that we could get
two Beanies.

Feeling suddenly smug, I took our prizes to a table in the
corner where Julianna and I could eat our Happy Meals. I
watched the lines grow longer and longer. I had to suppress
my desire to run over and tell the construction crew and the
nurse and the high school boys in line that today was the
first Teenie Beanie Baby Giveaway Day (they were obviously
clueless) and that they would never get back to work or
school on time.

Then I saw the mother with the frozen angry face.

She had been a pretty teenager, I was sure. Her blond hair
was pulled back into a ponytail, and she wore a gray college
sweatshirt and jeans. She had four children with her, their
ages somewhere between four and fourteen. But the thing
that was so striking was her face. The anger never left it. I
could tell that it wasn't just a momentary thing or even a
bad hair day. This was a woman who had lost her smile.
She looked deeply angry and unhappy, and her face
betrayed such deep scowl lines that I imagined that even
when she slept, the crevices remained.

I felt sad watching her. The kids alternated between acting
obnoxious and anxious. I could hear her sighs across the
room. She was *not* having fun. I wondered if she had read
the newspaper, if she had come in search of Teenie Beanies
for her children. And I wondered if, somewhere along the
way, she had stopped searching for her own dreams and
was now filled with resentment at her life.

I wondered too about my own face and the lines that I wear. When people looked at Julianna and me sitting in the corner of this very crowded McDonald's, did they see a woman who, at this moment in life, was content? Actually, on this day, they probably did. The absurdity of the whole scene—one hundred adults standing in line and another hundred children out on the play structure—made me smile. On another day, I might have been too impatient or frustrated to take it all in.

Julianna seemed happy enough with Twix the Giraffe and Doby the Doberman. But what she liked most of all (as did I) was eating our Happy Meals together. And I bet our faces showed it.

Contentment

Recently, a TV commercial caught my attention. It starts with quiet music, and then the camera does a close-up on a woman's face. She says, with deep feeling, "I don't know, I feel like something's missing. I just feel like there's a void . . . "

I stopped folding the laundry and watched to see what she would say next about this void. Then the woman points to her earlobe. "Right about here . . . " she adds. It's a commercial for diamond earrings.

The void isn't on our earlobes, and the ad people know that. They also know that most people experience an empty place inside, and the ad people use that fact to sell their products. Advertising exploits our longings as it tries to convince us that something glittery or glitzy or gigantic will fill that void.

And we keep on believing this message, telling ourselves that if only we could get that bigger house, car, paycheck or that smaller waist, mortgage, to-do list—then we'd arrive, we'd be happy and content. The only problem is that when we do get The Thing, the happiness lasts, if we're lucky, for about a week. When the excitement passes, we're stuck with ourselves again. And the cycle begins anew.

Whenever I experience what Buddhists refer to as Craving Mind, I find it helpful to use what I call the "fast-forward" technique. Let me give an example. I had a free hour between appointments last month, and I suddenly developed an urge to go shopping, specifically to buy some new candleholders for our Thanksgiving celebration. Without giving it much thought, I headed in the direction of the mall. But as I was about to get on the freeway, another part of me began to question why I was racing to get there and what it was that I really wanted. I began to "fast-forward" in my imagination and pictured myself arriving at the crowded mall, parking the car, walking around, buying candlesticks, and then hurrying to my next appointment. Then I saw myself several months later having to clean these candlesticks. Finally I pictured myself at some future point packing them up to donate to Goodwill.

I realized that this trip would deplete rather than restore my energy. I did not get on the freeway. I turned my car around, went to a local park, took out a blanket, and lay on the grass. As I closed my eyes, the breeze carried the sound of children's laughter my way, and the warm sun and earth relaxed me. I felt surrounded by a deep, peaceful presence.

When I finally arrived home, I remembered a pair of silver candlesticks that I had stored away. They had belonged to my grandmother, and we had never used them. I polished them with joy.

Contentment is not sold at any shopping mall. It doesn't come in any package. It arrives when we show up and pay attention to ourselves at the deepest level, when we get underneath the feelings that keep us frantically searching for ways to fill the void. We are most likely to find real contentment when we are willing to ask, "What is this longing really about?" and when we are willing to sit quietly and listen for the answers.

Tricycle

I've been practicing balance in my life, attempting to maintain my inner equilibrium when everything seems to try to throw me off center. Today I came across one Eastern philosophy's prescription: Practice chariot driving. That is a great image for what I am trying to develop—a way of staying upright in the driver's seat while life races on. It reminds me of something that happened sixteen years ago . . .

There I was in the bathroom, six months pregnant with Future Son #3, about to pull up the pants of Son #2, who had just proudly gone potty on his little chair. Unfortunately, I forgot that it would be wise (given that my body now resembled a Volkswagen) to use good body mechanics as I did so. I bent at what was left of my waist and felt a slight snap in my lower back. *Uh-oh,* I thought. There wasn't much pain, though, so I tried to straighten up. But I couldn't. I was stuck in an upside-down L-position. Son #2 thought this was pretty funny and ran away giggling, his pants only halfway up.

"Okay, this will pass in a second," I figured, standing there as if I were waiting for the gun to fire in the Olympic slalom ski event. After several minutes, I realized that I would not be standing upright anytime soon. Calculating that the toilet was within sitting range, I reached my hand over, put the lid down, and dropped onto the seat, my legs swinging up in the air.

Ten more minutes passed; my body simply would not cooperate in standing up. So I began to take stock of the situation: It was about nine o'clock in the morning. My husband would not return from work until six o'clock. I was alone in the house with a four-year-old and a two-year-old who could now do whatever they wanted, and I couldn't stop them. Not good.

I realized I had to do something. Somehow I needed to get to a phone. The only trouble was that this was in those blissful days before cell phones, and the nearest phone was down the hall, in our spare bedroom, about fifty feet away from the bathroom. Necessity is, as they say, the mother of invention, and a brilliant plan occurred to me.

"Boys," I called. "I need your help." Sons #1 and #2 came and stood next to giant mommy sitting on the toilet. "Now listen carefully. I want you to go out the back door, go down the steps, and get your tricycle. Then bring it in here to me," I carefully explained.

"But the rule is no bikes in the house," Son #1 just as carefully reminded me.

"Sweetie, this is an emergency. We're making an exception here. Go get your tricycle, pleeeaase?" Future Son #3 gave me a good solid kick.

The older brothers looked at one another, shrugged, and then went galloping down the hall. I had no idea if my plan was going to work.

I heard the back door open, then I heard some clanking, and soon I saw the boys proudly rolling the tricycle toward the bathroom.

"Now roll the bike over here next to me," I directed. It was a tight squeeze with all of us in there, but somehow I managed to get the tricycle in place between my legs. With a heave-ho, I pushed my immense behind onto the tiny trike seat.

The boys' eyes grew wide with a you've-got-to-be-kidding look, mixed with a hint of terror that their beautiful red tricycle would never be the same again.

"There!" I smiled. The Venus of Willendorf on wheels.

"Okay, sweeties. One more thing. Get behind me and push!"

Never had they seen their mother behaving so strangely. But this seemed like a fun new game, so they maneuvered behind me and started to push.

And so it was that the three of us (four, actually) began the trek toward the phone. Making our way down the long hallway and negotiating the turns required everything I knew, and then some, about keeping my balance. Leaning too far to the right or left would have resulted in my capsizing onto the floor. It required all of my attention (and all of my sense of humor!), but it all ended happily ever after. We arrived at the phone without tipping over, and I called my husband. I was still sitting on the trike when he arrived home forty-five minutes later. Then I spent the next two weeks in bed with a ruptured lower disk and the next fifteen years practicing correct back mechanics.

I smile as I think of my own little chariot.

Spiritual experiences often come in disguise. Not looking at all like our preconceived notions of a proper "spiritual" experience, an everyday event can bring with it an unexpected wealth of wisdom. My trike trip down the long hallway was a great illustration of how I might practice balance. It taught me other things as well:

• If we don't know the next step, we ought to keep an open mind. There is always a hidden solution to the problem at hand. Sometimes we have to remain in the "ambiguous spot" (read: "toilet") until the way shows itself.

• Limitation helps us to develop our creativity.

• Our ego thinks there's a straight line to success and wants us to look good getting there. The truth is that the straight line has lots of curves, and looking good takes second place to getting to the phone.

• If we just glance around, we'll receive all the help and support we need (often in the guise of little ones with big muscles).

• The vehicle for our change may look a lot like a tricycle even though we were hoping for something a little more elegant. And it probably won't make itself known until the instant we can make use of it.

• Finally, and most important, we should remember to bend at the knees.

Telephone Meditation, Take 2

Practicing telephone meditation can counter-act stress and depression and bring mindfulness into our daily lives.

Thich Nhat Hanh

The above quotation is from one of my favorite books by one of my favorite teachers, Buddhist monk Thich Nhat Hanh. His book *Peace Is Every Step* has meditations for everything—for sitting at traffic lights, for eating tangerines or cookies, for giving hugs. But there's one meditation that is giving me a little difficulty. It's his "Telephone Meditation."

This wise teacher's first recommendation is that when you hear the phone ring, you shouldn't move; just smile, breathe in and out, and on the first ring, recite this verse: "Listen, listen. This wonderful sound brings me back to my true self."

Maybe if I explain a typical day at my house, you'll understand the difficulty I'm having.

The phone rings. I happen to be, at that precise moment, in the middle of changing my two-year-old niece's particularly poopy diaper. Which goes to show that the First Universal Principle of Phone Calls and Kids still holds: When you're least able to answer the phone, it will ring.

Now, whenever I'm babysitting my niece, whom I love dearly, she has the habit of going poops exactly twenty minutes before my sister comes to pick her up. Just long enough that I can't pretend to not notice the smell and greet my sister with "Oops, she must have just gone."

So just when I'm finger-deep into this changing process, the phone rings. I think of breathing and smiling, but taking a deep breath is the last thing I want to do when changing a diaper of this particular variety.

The second ring. To follow the venerable monk's advice, I should at this point repeat the "Listen, listen . . . " verse. He believes my smile will become even more solid, and I'll be tension-free.

I don't think so. I realize I'd better answer the phone, because maybe it's my sister saying that she'll be back in two or three days and would I mind just a little if . . . Or maybe it's the call I've been expecting about a work project that is important to me. So I get up off the family room floor, telling my niece to stay still for a second while I get the phone.

It rings again. For the third ring, Thich Nhat Hanh has this advice: "When the phone rings for the third time, you can continue to practice breathing and smiling, as you walk to the phone slowly, with all your sovereignty. You are your own master."

Right. I do take a deep breath, albeit an exasperated one. I swoop up the phone just as my niece swoops up her diaper. With a grimace, I run to grab it from her, the contents plopping into patterns on the rug. Placing the receiver between my shoulder and my ear, I try to sound calm, centered, together. Zen-mama.

"Hello?"

It's the work call. I need to take it now. So while I attempt to clean up the mess, I try to negotiate the details of a workshop I'm supposed to lead next week.

At this point, my daughter and half-naked niece decide to get in a tugging match over a tiny doll, and the noise level grows. So I duck into the bathroom to wash my hands and lock the door behind me. Suddenly, there's a pounding on the door and loud cries of "M-o-o-m-m-m-y." That's when I remember the Second Universal Principle of Phone Calls and Kids: If you answer it, they will come.

I open the door, put my finger to my mouth to shush them, and move quickly into the kitchen. The girls are in hot pursuit. So I rely on the old food trick and grab little containers of crackers with cheese spread, packets of FruitiOs, and boxes of raisins, dropping them as I go, feeling like Indiana Jones attempting to thwart the bad guys who are chasing him. I run into the living room, hoping that I've lost them. My teenage son walks through the front door. "I'M H-O-O-O-M-E," he shouts. I cover the mouthpiece with one hand, contort my mouth into a "SH-H-HH," and point repeatedly toward the kitchen, hoping he understands all that to mean: *Please be quiet. I'm on the phone with an important call. Could you go take care of your sister and cousin?* Instead, he understands it to mean: *Great, Mom's on the phone. I can get the chips and watch Looney Toons in peace.*

The girls' pursuit is only slightly slowed by the snacks. As I start to move up the stairs, my daughter does the leghold. I try to shake her off, but to no avail. As I move back down the stairs, the doorbell rings. My sister is here to pick up her daughter. I open the door, give my sister a pleading look that means, *Please take the girls,* and then step out onto my porch, closing the door behind me. Unfortunately the connection on my cordless phone begins to break up, and I realize with horror that I need to go back inside in order to get rid of the static. It is then that I discover I've locked myself out.

That's when I give up. I shout into the receiver, "CAN I CALL YOU BACK A LITTLE LATER?" not knowing if the caller hears me. I turn off the phone and lean my head against the door.

So you see my difficulty. Thich Nhat Hanh writes, "You don't have to go into a meditation hall to do this wonderful practice of meditation. You can do it . . . at home."

I'm still trying.

III
Music Lessons

*Those who do not know how to sing
and dance
will never reach God.*

Bapuji

It was one of those glorious Sundays in September when the entire state of California comes out for summer's last hurrah. With school and work and jackets right around the corner, we all wanted to hold on to the freedom of warm days just a little longer. And so it was no surprise that hundreds of other people had the same idea our family had—to drive over the hill to go to the beach.

As it happened, it was also the weekend of the annual Capitola Art and Wine Festival—a beachfront celebration with a glorious mix of colors, music, and movement. We made our way through the streets, walking past booths filled with the creations of artisans. We ate crab cakes and sipped wine. We sat on the stone wall that separates the city from the sand and watched people and waves and seagulls. But the best part of the day came when I was standing in line for the restroom.

Since it was the line for the women's restroom, it was naturally a very long line. It wound out of the blue brick building, down the sidewalk, and along the grassy knoll that overlooked the beach. Normally I'd have sighed at the length of the wait, but this day was so beautiful, with the sun and the breeze and the diamonds of light reflecting off of the ocean, that I actually smiled as I took my place at the end of the line.

There was a stage set up on the grass near us, and a band was preparing to play. An announcement was made that a children's group from a local dance school was going to perform an African dance. Twenty barefoot kids, ranging in age from six to sixteen, took their places, smiling and excited. And then the drummers began to beat their drums.

As these drumbeats reverberated in the air, it was as if a great wave, a deep and primitive life force, began to move through the crowd. I watched this wave move through the children's dance group as their feet pounded the earth. Then I saw it flow into the naked babies nearby. They had stopped their toddling when the music first started, but soon were squealing with delight as they recognized the beat. They lifted their unsteady feet and waved their arms, falling and laughing, ecstatic in the dance. The music coursed through young people, old people, women in thong bikinis, scruffy-faced men holding small brown bags. All the bodies within earshot of the drums were caught up in the power of the music and could only respond with the movement of dance.

In our bathroom line, the seventy-year-old woman in front of me, who was wearing a green tank top and shorts, moved her brown and crinkly arms back and forth. The wave coursed through the two women behind me, tourists with large white hats and Southern accents; first they started tapping their toes, and soon they were swaying their hips. My own body began to let go as something freed up inside of me. Forgetting that I do not usually dance in public, I let the music have its way.

I looked around at all of us moving and smiling, caught up in a great and joyful dance. In our more somber moments we might not choose some of these folks as dance partners, but the Spirit in the music wouldn't let anyone remain separate. It wove us together and aligned us with our true nature, with our deep and ancient and connected human selves.

That day was a reminder to me of the power of music. In our modern age, we are only beginning to understand the physical and emotional effects of music. But indigenous cultures have always known and valued its power. Anthropologist Angeles Arrien has studied many such cultures, and she has found that they assess health in ways very different from ours. Instead of taking temperatures or running blood tests, they ask four basic questions: *Where in your life did you stop singing? Where in your life did you stop dancing? Where in your life did you stop being enchanted by stories? And where in your life did you become uncomfortable with the sweet territory of silence?* They believe that where you stopped singing, or where you stopped dancing, or where you stopped being enchanted with stories, or where you became uncomfortable with silence is where you began to experience soul loss and illness.

> In our more somber moments we might not choose some of these folks as dance partners, but the Spirit in the music wouldn't let anyone remain separate.

These questions give me pause. They help me to touch places within myself that have been blocked, places where I do not feel whole or well. When I ask these questions in regard to my family—Where in our life did *we* stop dancing?—I get clues as to the health of my family and can recognize areas where we might need to adjust our busy schedules. And if I ask them in regard to our society, I get even more insight as to why we do not seem to be collectively well.

Such questions are not seen as very important in our society. Music and dance and storytelling and silence are the first things to get dropped from our children's school curricula. If we as parents don't pick up the missing pieces, our children will not flourish. They will be left without anchors, without the joy of celebration, without the ability to make myths or magic or meaning.

Because I do not want us to experience such soul loss, I invite those I love to sing, dance, light candles, bless one another, tell stories, sit in silence. We honor in ritual those major life passages—birth, coming of age, leaving home, illness, and death—and we honor the daily rituals of grace before meals, bedtime prayer, and hugs and kisses. We turn up the music and dance, in the kitchen or living room, dancing cha-cha or hip-hop or just twirling in circles. And we don't let the fact that half of us are tone-deaf stop us from singing. It is in these moments of singing and dancing, praying and storytelling that we feel God moving through us, making us whole.

Vocation

When I was a kid, I didn't know what I wanted to be when I grew up. I knew I liked certain things: horses, reading, writing poems, and drawing for hours on end. I also loved to write plays, and I'd coerce my siblings and all the little girls in the neighborhood to act them out. These would be elaborate performances. I'd string Christmas lights around doorways, paint all the lightbulbs in our living room lamps bright red, and painstakingly print out playbills for the audience—which consisted of my mother and whatever other kids I could drag in.

But when I was around eight or nine, one of my most favorite things to do was to act out the Mass. I had a crush on Jimmy Carelli, a devout Catholic boy who lived down the street. He was a year older than I was and, more important, an altar boy with real-life experience in the sanctuary. As a girl, I was forbidden such access. I promised Jimmy that if he came to my house to play Mass, he could be the priest. He was a bit reluctant, afraid it might be some sort of a sin. After I convinced him that even if it *was* a sin he could confess it next week, he agreed.

We would set up the living room to look like a church. One of the red lightbulbs left over from that week's neighborhood play would become the sanctuary flame. We'd cover the coffee table with my mother's white tablecloth, and it would serve as a fine altar. On top of the cloth we would set a vase of plastic flowers, a candle, and a crucifix. We'd borrow a wine goblet from the kitchen cupboard, fill it with grape juice, and sneak a small china plate from my grandmother's collection. We would convert my dad's bathrobe into a vestment for Jimmy, and we'd find a bell to ring during the consecration. Finally, we would take slices of Wonder Bread, and with the top from one of my little sister's baby food jars, we'd cut out circles of bread to use as hosts.

Jimmy came as close to a real priest as I could imagine. He even knew Latin, having memorized his responses as an altar boy. When he held up the bread and the wine, I would enthusiastically ring the bell. At communion, we would swallow our little hosts with great reverence, trying not to chew, and we would bow our heads in prayer for long periods—or at least until we got the giggles. Then Jimmy would bestow the blessing, "*In nomine Patris, et Filii, et Spiritus Sancti.*"

But Jimmy never knew what happened after he left. I'd walk him to the door and, with a smile, wave good-bye. Then I'd go back to the altar and, making sure no one was watching, pick the bathrobe up off the floor and put it on. I'd cut out a few more hosts and pour a little more grape juice. And then, in my living room, I would do the unthinkable: *I* would say Mass, this time as the priest.

❖

Fifteen years later, I was taking those career interest inventories, trying to figure out what I wanted to be when I grew up. But childhood dreams have a way of lingering on at the edge of our lives, calling out in fairly irrational voices for us to pay attention to them and, God help us, even pursue them. I guess that's how I explain how I found myself in a Catholic seminary at age twenty-three, one of two women in a class of all men who were studying for the priesthood.

As the Yentl of the Catholic set, I kept asking the same irritating questions—such as "Why would I be given wings, if not to fly?" I figured the institutional church would get around to changing the rules about women's ordination any day now, and when it did, I'd be ready with my nice little Master of Divinity degree. Ah, the optimism of youth.

Being a woman in a primarily male institution had some interesting moments. During the first two years, I commuted more than fifty miles each way to go to classes. I would drive my car to BART, our local commuter train, ride up to Berkeley, transfer to a shuttle van that took me to the top of the hill, and then walk several more blocks to class. This

> As the Yentl of the Catholic set, I kept asking the same irritating questions— such as "Why would I be given wings, if not to fly?"

was particularly challenging when I was newly pregnant and had morning sickness. My first class was at 8:00 A.M., which meant that I had to leave my apartment at 6:00 A.M. I'd bring my books, along with a cup of tea, soda crackers, and a large baggie or two, hoping I didn't gross out other passengers too much. After the train ride, I'd race to the shuttle bus, take it to the top of the hill, then run up another hill to class, stopping off in a bathroom to throw up one last time. I'd arrive at my seat just before the professor began to speak. I must admit I was just a teeny bit miffed when a few of my classmates would wander into class ten or twenty minutes late, sipping their coffee and winking at the professor. They lived in the rooms above the classroom, on the second floor of the same building—a tough commute, to be sure!

The three Catholic seminaries at the school hadn't quite worked out a few kinks that developed with the arrival of women. Take the preaching class, for example. I showed up on the first day, ready to learn how to deliver great sermons. By then, I was getting used to being the only woman and the only noncleric in a class. But in this class, I was just a little intimidated by the fact that I was the only one not wearing a long white cassock. However, I planned to stay in the class, until I found out that women were not allowed in the sanctuary of the church where we were supposed to preach for our final exam. The professor hadn't faced this dilemma before, and he became somewhat agitated, complaining that he'd have to arrange a separate gathering so that I could preach. I solved his problem and dropped the class.

And there was one other priest-prof who was not very nice. He assigned us a reflection paper on what it meant to be a minister, and when I wrote mine using feminine pronouns (it was, after all, *my* experience I was reflecting upon), he took a large red pen and crossed out every single *she* and wrote *he*. He went out of his way to write a note explaining that *he* was the correct pronoun to use in all cases and that I should not forget that. I never did.

The only other class I chose not to take was "Sacraments." I was eight months pregnant at the time, and I didn't think I could fit into any of the albs that the priests-to-be were supposed to wear as they practiced acting out the sacraments. I thought of my father's bathrobe and smiled. I decided to catch that class the next time it came around.

Overall, the years in seminary were among the best in my life. We moved closer to the school for my last two years, which greatly improved my mood. I loved learning about Scripture and grace and justice. And it was immensely gratifying to put what I was learning into practice, working with people, directing retreats, designing ritual.

But I must admit that the highlight came in the middle of my third year. The men in my class were preparing to be ordained as deacons, the step before their ordination as priests. The women in the class (there were now three of us) were not, by virtue of our gender, eligible for this rite. We talked about participating in a silent protest that some other men and women were organizing, which consisted of passing out daisies at the church and standing during the sermon. I wasn't sure I wanted to attend.

But I was not the one who decided how I spent that evening. Sometimes events happen in such a way that it feels as if the universe is validating your dreams, saying yes to you as you say yes to your path. You see, I was nine months pregnant at the time. On the night of my class's ordination, my water broke, and I gave birth to my first child.

And so here I sit, twenty years later, no longer wondering what I'm going to be when I grow up. I've arrived. And guess what? My childhood dreams have come true.

For two decades, I have broken bread, poured grape juice, preached, prayed, told stories, bestowed blessings, taken care of the sick, heard confessions. I have been a parent. These have been the sacraments of my daily life and, I suspect, of yours. These are simple, sacred acts. These are how we mediate love, as we minister to our own little congregations—children, spouse, family, and friends.

I have discovered that it is a great vocation.

Duck Day

Recently I attended a workshop in which the presenter asked us to break into small groups and tell one another stories of hope. A woman in her sixties was in my group, and she had us enthralled with this story of her special family tradition . . .

One Good Friday, more than thirty years ago, a young Catholic mom did what all good Catholic moms did back then on Good Friday: she packed up her four children and went to church for noon services.

Now this happened to be a particularly beautiful day, and the four young children were in a particularly feisty mood, not at all cooperative with the adult agenda of sitting on a hard pew in a dark church. It didn't help that everything looked different, that all the statues had been draped in purple velvet cloth and that incense was clouding up the air. After she chased one son down the aisle three times while holding her crying infant, and after breaking up a finger-flicking match that her other two kids were having under the pew, this mother made a difficult decision. She gathered her children together and spoke to them in a hoarse whisper.

"We're leaving *now.*"

With the baby under one arm and dragging the other three kids behind her, she sheepishly walked down the center aisle, hoping nobody would notice. The other parishioners collectively sighed a prayer of thanksgiving.

She pushed and pulled the kids to the car. She felt slightly sacrilegious when she announced that they were leaving church and going to the park.

"Forgive me, God, but maybe outdoors we can all pray a little easier."

They went to a local park that had a pond with lots and lots of ducks. She found a half-smashed package of saltines under her car's backseat, and she and her children spent Good Friday feeding and chasing the ducks.

A year passed, and Good Friday came around once again. This time, Mom felt just a tiny twinge of guilt as she made the decision to skip the church scene and go directly to the park, with stale bread in hand. The children were overjoyed and bounced out of the car as soon as they parked.

Yet another year passed, and this time Mom didn't think twice. Prayer would be with the ducks, and that was that.

"Okay, kids, it's Duck Day. Get in the car!"

Every year from that point on, Good Friday, or rather, Duck Day, found Mom and the kids hanging out at the park. The children started inviting friends along, and soon other parents joined in, everyone wanting to find out what this Duck Day was all about. Some years it rained, but the ceremony went on anyway. The cars pulled up near the pond, and the children raced out and threw pieces of bread. Then, soaking wet, they plopped back into their cars. There was even one year when the unimaginable happened. It had been raining so hard that there were *no* ducks in sight. They had all just disappeared. Stunned, the children stared out through the raindrops on the car windows. After a minute, one of the boys (a teenager by now) jumped out into the rain, bent his arms into wings, and began to waddle and quack like a duck. Screaming with delight, the other children poured out of their cars. Some became ducks; some threw bread. The sacrament was complete.

The years went by. Sometimes twenty people showed up, sometimes seventy-five or more. Duck Day became one of the most important days on the community's calendar. The mother's children grew up and left home, but they still managed to be home for the big holidays—Thanksgiving, Christmas, and Duck Day. Three got married and now brought children of their own; the numbers just kept growing.

And so it was that last year more than 150 people, young and old, gathered at a small pond in Northern California to celebrate death, resurrection, and Duck Day.

I think Jesus would be pleased.

Invisible Friends

A few years ago we added a new member to our family. She doesn't eat much, and even though she's extremely quiet, she teaches us a lot.

I was introduced to her one day while I was reading the morning paper. Julianna, then two and a half years old, tugged at the sleeve of my robe.

"Mama, I have a new friend."

"Oh, really?" I asked. "Where is this friend?"

"Right *here*," she said, impatient at my inability to see beyond my nose.

"Oh. Of course." I wasn't sure what to ask next. "Is it a boy or a girl?" I ventured.

"A girl!" Julianna retorted.

"What's her name?" I asked.

Julianna tipped her head as if listening for the answer. Then she replied, "It's Abba."

I raised my eyebrows in surprise. I had never used this word around her. As you may know, in some languages,

like Aramaic, it is the word for daddy or papa. It is also a
name that Jesus used in addressing God.

Two things immediately went through my mind. First, I was
delighted to discover that Abba was a girl. Second, I began to
wonder if the doorbell would ring and a bunch of Tibetan
monks would enter to take Julianna away as a reincarnated
lama of one sort or another. (I had just watched the movie
Little Buddha, and my imagination got a little carried away.)

I was so impressed by Julianna's obvious connection with
the spiritual realm that I called to tell a friend the name of
my daughter's invisible companion.

"Is that so?" my friend said upon hearing this. "Well, when
my son was three, he had an invisible friend too."

"Oh, *really?* Well, what was *his* friend's name?" I asked.

"Poopy."

It seems to me that human beings are hardwired for having
invisible friends. They show up in every culture and make
their way into our sacred texts. Angels and other divine
messengers are always showing up to let us know that
we'll miss a whole lot if we focus only on the solid and
three-dimensional.

Just the other day, as I was thinking about Abba, I happened
upon this story by Rumi, the thirteenth-century Sufi poet. I

smiled with delight and kept looking over my shoulder as I
read it:

> A village woman once was walking by Muhammad.
> She thought he was just an ordinary illiterate.
> She didn't believe that he was a prophet.
>
> She was carrying a two-month-old baby.
> As she came near Muhammad, the baby turned
> and said, "Peace be with you, Messenger of God."
>
> The mother cried out, surprised and angry,
> "What are you saying,
> and how can you suddenly talk!"
>
> The child replied, "God taught me first,
> and then Gabriel."
>   "Who is this Gabriel?
> I don't see anyone."
>   "He is above your head,
> Mother. Turn around. He has been telling me
> many things."
>   "Do you really see him?"
>   "Yes."

As her little one continues to speak, the mother enters into
the same state of knowing as her baby. Rumi concludes,

> When God gives this knowing,
> inanimate stones, plants, animals, everything,
> fills with unfolding significance.

It's stories like this that remind me to take the existence of
Abba seriously. Sometimes we set a place for her at dinner,

or we throw her a birthday party. She's taught me that just because I can't see or touch some things, it doesn't mean that they don't exist. She's taught me to play with boundaries, to be curious about unseen energies, to be open to invisible support. I will give you a few more examples, and then you can decide what to believe.

One day, Julianna was outside of church, balancing on top of a brick planter that was more than two feet high. I hurried over, afraid that she'd fall. "Honey, be careful," I said.

"It's okay. Abba is holding my hand." She smiled and continued walking with absolute confidence.

It was a wonderful picture of what it looks like to trust in grace.

> She's taught me that just because I can't see or touch some things, it doesn't mean that they don't exist.

As I was putting Julianna to bed recently, she asked me to leave her room so that she could pray in private. I was surprised at her request; I left the room, but I couldn't resist peeking around the door to see what was happening. I saw her kneeling on her bed, her eyes closed, her hands folded in a perfect prayer position, facing a battery-powered lantern that was glowing on her headboard. (She and her dad had taken the lantern out the week before when they had camped in the backyard.) She looked angelic.

After she was finished, Julianna yelled out that it was okay for me to come back in. I asked her where she had learned to pray that way.

"Abba taught me," she said quietly. I believed her.

One day, as we were driving to Toys "R" Us, Julianna called to me from the backseat.

"Mama?"

"What, sweetie?"

"I know where love is."

"Really? Where?" I asked.

"It's in your heart. Try this. Hold your breath, and put your hand on your chest. Do you feel it beating?"

I did as instructed. "Yes, I feel it."

"Love is right where the beat is. When you feel the beat— that's where love is."

Somewhat amazed, I asked, "How do you know this?"

"Abba told me. She crawled into my crib when we were both babies and told me that love is in the beat of your heart."

It's difficult to focus on driving when such messages are coming from the backseat.

Lest you think Abba is a complete innocent, let me set the record straight. Abba has made her share of messes around here, including scribbling on a wall or two. She doesn't always play games fairly, which frustrates Julianna. And sometimes Abba gets angry and moves back to her other home, which is okay, since then we don't have to worry about sitting on her.

Abba is not the only invisible friend we have around here, but she is the primary one. Others have shown up over the years, but they have come and gone. We also have angels living in our house, but they only come out at night. Julianna says that they dance in her room, and when they do, sparkles fill the air. So it was no surprise to me when I heard a radio interview yesterday in which a well-known religious teacher suggested that if people find formal meditation difficult, they might simply go into their child's room at night and meditate on the angels that are dancing through the air.

Sadly, I suspect that one day soon, Julianna will say there's no such thing as invisible friends. Abba and the angels will disappear. But maybe, just maybe, we will continue to feel the gentlest of touches or the quietest of presences, and we will realize that we are not alone. And maybe Abba will continue to give us a way of knowing, one in which stones, plants, animals, and everything fills with unfolding significance.

Bedtime Blessings

I see ritual when people sit together
silently by an open fire.
Remembering.
As human beings have remembered for
thousands and thousands of years.

Robert Fulghum

We all know about the passage of time. It moves through our days, through our bodies, through our lives. Time can seem to move slowly, almost imperceptibly. You might notice little signs: your child's footed sleeper is getting snugger, your daughter no longer calls you "Mama," your lower back is more fragile. Or time can seem to move all too quickly: children leave home, parents die, friends get sick. Try as we might, there is no stopping this movement of time. It pulls us and those we love onward. Our part is to learn to flow gracefully with it.

As we go through our days, we receive many blessings and we experience great longings. Perhaps we give voice to these in prayer—in words of gratitude or in cries of petition. We do not *have* to pray; God does not require this of us. Rather, prayer is for *our* sake. It works on *us*, helping us to feel connected to a larger reality. Prayer teaches us how to let go, how to allow the passage of time to flow through extended and grateful hands.

A natural time for prayer, especially prayer with children, is at bedtime, at the transition from light to darkness. It is a time when parents throughout the ages, in all religious traditions, have tucked in their little ones with rituals of storytelling and kisses and prayers, letting their children know that even in the great darkness they can feel safe.

My children are the ones who asked that bedtime prayer be one of the rituals woven into our family life. In the Advent season when my three boys were only two, four, and six years old, I brought out an Advent wreath. During those long nights of winter, when we waited and longed for the return of the sun, we sat together at bedtime to light the candles. The boys raced through the house, turning out all the lights so as to get the full effect of the candle-light. We sang Christmas songs and said our prayers. It was a magical time.

And then Christmas came and went, and I packed away the candles and the wreath. Bedtime now was a more solitary affair; I tucked them in and said prayers with each boy in his own bed. They were disappointed. They didn't understand why we weren't gathering in the living room and singing and praying together. They wanted Advent to continue.

And so began our family ritual. I bought a small oil lamp, and each night we cleared the coloring books from the coffee table, turned off all the lights, and in the darkness, struck a match. Immediately the boys grew quiet, watching the flame dance in front of them. Once again, we all knew that our day was ending, that we were all home safe and sound. We felt held together in the darkness and in the light; we were learning that both are the home of God.

> Prayer teaches us how to let go, how to allow the passage of time to flow through extended and grateful hands.

It was harder to think of "spiritual" songs to sing outside of Christmastime; the most frequent requests were "Twinkle, Twinkle, Little Star" and "How Much Is That Doggy in the Window?" These worked nicely. After we sang, we sat—sometimes in quiet, sometimes in silliness—and remembered those things for which we were grateful and those things for which we hoped.

"Thank you, God, that I caught that fly ball," voiced Ben. "Thank you, God, for my family and friends" was Matthew's nightly prayer. We prayed for months for David's pet rat, Ratical, who had died unexpectedly. Often we prayed for peace in the world and for the children who didn't have enough food. Sometimes we just sat.

What was most important, we came to realize, was not so much the words we used or the songs we sang as the fact that we were gathered together as a family at the end of our very busy days—days that soon became months, months that soon became years—to share with one another and give thanks for even the smallest things in our lives. It was a ritual that helped us to experience something that is already there—a great Presence in our midst, patiently waiting for us to open our hearts.

If you had stood in the darkness and peeked in our window back then, you would've seen three little boys in pajamas singing their hearts out. If you had looked ten years later, those boys would have been teens in baggy pants, and a new little soul would have been sitting on one of their laps. The boys would have been sitting in silence, smiling as their little sister rushed to blow out the candle, just as they themselves once had.

I am grateful for what my children have taught me about prayer. Sitting with them has changed me; I pray that it works its transformative power on them as well. I have the sense that it does. Just last week, as we drove home from church, Julianna's eyes were tightly closed. Paul asked her if she was falling asleep. "No, Daddy," she answered. "I'm just closing my eyes to see the flame inside."

I pray that no matter where time leads my children, they will always be able to sing and pray and find light in the darkness, experiencing themselves at home in the Sacred Presence that surrounds them.

Potato Stories

*Of course, we don't have a spiritual exaltation
every time we pick up a potato.*

Susan Wittig Albert

ONE POTATO: BUMPING POTATOES
I am sitting here in the church pew, surrounded by people
who are, in everyday life, engineers, kindergarten teachers,
salespeople, surgeons, lawyers, CEOs, unemployed, secre-
taries, moms, dads, grandparents, single folks, widows, and
children. But in here, we are simply a little community of
ordinary people journeying together in faith.

I've tried to live without such a community. It was easy to
stay in my nice isolated world and not have to deal with the
inevitable irritations and difficulties that arise when strangers
come together. But this isolation eventually caught up with
me, and I realized that self-sufficiency is overrated. I missed
the stories, the rituals, the examples of compassion and kindness, the companionship of others. I missed having a spiritual home, a place where people help each other find God.

So here I am in this pew. It's not always comfortable.
Community is a mirror, one in which we will see our best face
and our worst. A spiritual community is not only the place
where we go about the work of transforming the world; it
is also the place of *our* transformation. Sometimes I'd rather
interact only with certain people, especially with those who
think like me or act in ways I approve of. But growth requires
that I move out of my narrow and separate world.

The experience of being in a community reminds me of the
practice in Korea of washing potatoes. I read that in that
country, when people want to wash a lot of dirty potatoes,
they don't wash them one at a time. They put
them *all* in a tub of water. Then they put a
stick in the tub and move it up and down,
causing the potatoes to bump up against one
another. As they bump into one another, the
hard dirt covering them is loosened and falls
off. It would take a long time to wash these
potatoes one by one; by putting them all
together, they help to clean one another.

> A spiritual community is not only the place where we go about the work of transforming the world; it is also the place of *our* transformation.

This is why I choose to be in a community of faith. When we
join hands, our prayers and our lives bump up against one
another, and something holy is made in the process.

TWO   POTATO: FORGIVENESS
My two nieces were over at my house last week, and they
were having a fight. Christine, age nine, was very angry
with her five-year-old sister, Amelia. Christine stormed
upstairs and didn't come down for more than an hour. Finally

my sister called her to come and talk with us. She came down reluctantly, unwilling to let go of her anger. Her mom gently reminded her of the potato story that she had been told at school. When I looked puzzled, my sister recited the story. After hearing it again, Christine decided to forgive Amelia.

The story, which was written by an unknown author, is posted on a number of Web sites. It reads as follows:

> One of my teachers had each one of us bring a clear plastic bag and a sack of potatoes. For every person we'd refuse to forgive in our life experience, we were told to choose a potato, write on it the name and date, and put it in the plastic bag. Some of our bags, as you can imagine, were quite heavy.
>
> We were then told to carry this bag with us everywhere for one week, putting it beside our bed at night, on the car seat when driving, next to our desk at work.
>
> The hassle of lugging this around with us made it clear what a weight we were carrying spiritually and how we had to pay attention to it all the time to not forget and keep leaving it in embarrassing places.
>
> Naturally, the condition of the potatoes deteriorated to a nasty slime. This was a great metaphor for the price we pay for keeping our pain and heavy negativity!

Too often we think of forgiveness as a gift to
the other person, and it clearly is for ourselves!

So the next time you decide you can't forgive
someone, ask yourself . . . Isn't MY bag heavy
enough?

THREE POTATO: THE MEASURE WE USE

A friend of ours, Fr. Seàn, worked in Kenya years ago,
and he shared with us an image he used with the people
there to help them understand the line from the Our
Father that says, "Forgive us our debts as we also have
forgiven our debtors."

In Kenya, the women used old gasoline containers with the
tops cut off as measuring devices. These tin cans were about
eighteen inches high and held about four and a half gallons
of gas. The women used them to measure out the grain or
potatoes they were selling at the market. The word the
people used for these cans is *debe.*

The women who were selling grain filled their *debes* to
overflowing, shook them so that all the grain settled, and
then poured more grain on top. What they ended up with
were containers in full measure, "pressed down, shaken
together, running over." But for some unknown reason, the
women who were selling potatoes beat in the sides and the
bottoms of their cans, creating "crushed *debes.*" When
these women poured the potatoes into their *debes,* a large
potato would often get wedged above the bottom of the

can, leaving a large empty space below it. This allowed only ten or eleven potatoes to be placed on top of it, short-changing the customer.

Fr. Seàn used this example from the people's daily life to help them understand the gospel. He would tell them, "The *debe* you use with another is the *debe* you need to use when you come before God. When you go before God with a big *debe*, asking God to fill it, and the next day your brother or sister comes to you asking you for forgiveness or for something they need, and you bring out the *crushed debe*, then don't go back to God with the big one the next time."

The message was clear: Don't take in one measure and then give in another, for the measure you give will be the measure you get back. And you will be forgiven in the same measure that you forgive.

FOUR: MENTAL PROLIFERATION
This is a story by meditation teacher Leigh Brasington that illustrates how the mind takes the simplest thought, jumps on it, and runs off in all directions.

When I read this story, my first reaction was "Ouch." It hits very close to home. How often I get all worked up over something that is entirely a creation of my own thinking! Enough said.

> A woman wants some potatoes for the meal she is cooking, so she sends her husband to the marketplace to buy potatoes. As he walks out the door, she calls after him, "Be sure and get a

good price." So all the way to the marketplace, the man is thinking about potatoes and what he'll have to pay. If he buys the very best potatoes, he knows he'll have to pay more than if he buys lesser quality potatoes. On the other hand, the lesser quality potatoes are just that— not so good. In fact he knows he'll have to be very careful in buying other than top price potatoes because the seller might try to stick him with a bad potato, even a rotten potato. When he thinks of someone cheating him by giving him a rotten potato, he gets really mad. "Why do people have to be so greedy as to stick me with a rotten potato?" Just at this point he reaches the stall of the potato seller and screams at him, "You can keep your rotten potatoes!" and walks off.

The Mother of Men

On this otherwise ordinary night at the end of July, the men in my life are out under the stars beating drums in a redwood forest.

Okay, actually, *I'm* the one with the drum. But I thought drumming sounded more dramatic than "the men in my life are out under the stars eating steaks in a redwood forest."

Yesterday, my husband, his best friend, my two brothers-in-law, and five teenage boys packed up the minivans and headed out for what is now the annual Men's Weekend. This tradition began six years ago when our oldest son, Ben, turned thirteen. Puberty was turning Ben inside out, stretching him, changing his voice and his biceps, morphing him into an adult before our eyes. We wanted to find some way to mark this transition, to celebrate this passage by giving him a blessing.

Some men never hear their father's stories or receive their father's blessing. They do not hear their elders say: *We see you. Your life is important. What you say should be heard.* Perhaps I am overly sensitized to this. Over and over in therapy sessions, I hear about what life is like for people who've never received a blessing from their parents. They walk around with an empty space inside, usually looking in all the wrong places for the message that they are good and whole and blessed.

There is no ready-made formula for giving such a blessing. Life in our American melting pot often lacks meaningful rituals. Most of our ancestors' wisdom has been boiled away, replaced with bland consumerism. But by borrowing from one tradition and taking from another, we were able to piece together a ritual in which Ben could be blessed.

The older men would take Ben camping in a redwood forest. They would go on hikes, build fires, and talk into the night. My husband, who had been reading a number of books about men's psychology, wrote out a list of questions intended to spark conversation on what it means to be a man. The questions covered such topics as intimacy, power, heroes, fears, dreams, work, women. I heard that the sharing was richer and deeper than any had imagined it would be. My son looked older when he returned; he looked as if he had taken in a blessing. And the older men looked as if they had bestowed a blessing and had been blessed in return.

That first weekend was six years ago. Since then, three other boys have reached the age of thirteen, and now each of them attends subsequent weekends as one of the elders. On this July night, the fifth boy is receiving his blessing. He is being seen for who he is and is getting the message that who he is matters. He is listening to stories about what it means to be a man and is beginning to understand that his story is part of a larger story. In the telling of the tales, something solid is being made.

I don't think it's an accident that all this is happening under redwood trees. We are fortunate to live near the California coast, where redwoods have grown for twenty million years. These trees have trunks that are incredibly strong, resistant to fire, insects, and disease. They often grow close together, their roots intertwined like fingers, providing them stability despite their great height. I imagine that bits of redwood bark and needles fall down upon this little group of men, getting in hair and tents and shoes. Perhaps these giants of the forest are imparting some part of their great strength, adding depth and breadth and height to these human beings who've come to visit.

All I know is that when the men return, it will seem as if they've internalized the forest. Smelling of smoke and perspiration, my teenage men will wrap their long branchy arms around my shoulder and say, "It was good." When I ask for more details, they'll just smile, give a little squeeze, and repeat in a deep and rooted voice, "It was good."

They'll have been gone just forty-eight hours, and I'll try to piece together some of what those hours held. I'll develop the roll of film at Longs, then scour the pictures for information. If it's anything like last year, I'll see a photo of eight males walking shirtless, their shirts tied around their heads and their shorts pulled down extra low, the older men showing their underwear in solidarity with the teens. I'll hear stories of daylong hikes, of Ranger Bob coming four times to quiet the camp, of campfire breakfasts of bacon and fresh coffee. I'll hear that the young men were eloquent as they spoke of love and God and life. I'll see sunburned noses and dirty vans. I'll smell smoke on their jackets and hair and sleeping bags, and I'll refuse to do the laundry. But I'll change my mind, and then I'll smile when I find bits of redwood clinging to their clothes.

❖

I am filled with a deep peace, grateful that my sons have interconnected roots with these older men. My sons know that they'll never be alone; they know that they have men in their lives with whom they can share struggles and joys. I witness this connection in the long, deep hugs and pats on the back that they give one another as they leave to go home.

Like the redwoods, these young men will grow straight and tall. They will take in the blessing and they will blossom, and, in turn, they will bless the world. They already tell me that they will do this ritual for their sons.

I too am blessed.

I am the mother of men.

Perhaps these giants of the forest are imparting some part of their great strength, adding depth and breadth and height to these human beings who've come to visit.

The list of questions created for the first Men's Weekend can be found in an appendix at the back of this book.

Married

On the outside we looked innocent enough: a middle-aged couple driving away from the pier in a dusty 1994 Toyota Corolla. But underneath the surface was a wild and pulsing energy that could reemerge at any moment.

Paul gave me a kiss when we stopped at a light. Our tenth anniversary getaway was coming to an end. We had only been gone twenty-eight hours, yet it seemed a blissful eternity. The light changed, and we began the trek from Half Moon Bay back to Silicon Valley—with live Dungeness crabs crawling in the trunk of our car.

As it turned out, we were the only guests at the bed-and-breakfast on that Friday evening in early December. A wedding party had booked the whole place for the following night, and apparently nobody else had wanted to stay only one night. The B&B was an old country inn with a saloon on the first floor and the bedrooms on the second and third. Christmas decorations transformed the place into a magical world, with angels hanging from banisters and the smell of evergreen branches filling the air. When we opened the door to our bedroom, we were delighted to discover a private bath with a claw-footed tub, fresh flowers on the antique dresser, and a four-poster brass bed with chocolates on the pillows.

It took a while before I fully arrived. My body was there, but I was not entirely in it. The constant inner dialogue of daily life was still chattering in my head. With kids and the usual hectic pace of life, it takes some time for me to slow down, to come back to quiet and to my love.

Ever so slowly, we moved into our bodies. As we held each other, we felt energy moving all the way through us, spreading warmth, flowing out of our fingers and toes. We felt life in its fullness as we talked and touched and laughed. Then we looked at each other and said, as we always do at these times, "Why don't we do this more often?"

We walked in the quiet beauty of a night lit up with tiny white lights. The music of Christmas floated out of open doors, filling us with the spirit of the holiday. Paul took my hand and I got a little shiver; I couldn't believe that after so many years it felt so new and raw, so close.

We went into one store and then another in search of a Christmas ornament. This is an annual event; it began on our honeymoon, when we were on the island of Kauai. We brought home an ornament of a little kissing hula couple, placing it on our tree along with our memories. Each year we search for one that symbolizes our love. Most of the time it is a joy to do, but there was one year when we were in the middle of an argument. On that anniversary, we had no child care and little money. We went out to dinner at a local coffee shop and ate scrambled eggs and potatoes.

Then I went by myself to Cost Plus and picked out an ornament. When I got home, it broke.

But this year, we were good. Our hours together stretched out before us, and we had, as they say, "quality time."

Not that I have anything against "quantity time" with Paul—all those hours of cooking, cleaning, shopping. On most days, I love the sense of companionship I feel as the two of us go about doing what needs to be done. But eventually, months and months of errands and housekeeping and parenting take their toll, and I lose touch—literally—with my husband, and with myself. It's hard to do anything other than throw on my flannel nightgown and drop into bed, fantasizing only about sleep. We give each other a kiss and whisper, "Maybe early in the morning."

That's when I know it's time for us to get away together, if only for a night.

On Saturday morning we had a leisurely breakfast, sipping the best coffee we had ever tasted. Then we went for a drive along the coast, circling back inland to visit the extraordinary general store in the tiny town of San Gregorio. Built in 1889, this store has kerosene lanterns, saddles, toys, great books, and home-baked treats. We bought some Christmas gifts for the family and listened to a group dressed in medieval attire playing Celtic holiday music. Couples danced in the aisles. Even Paul and I were entranced enough to do a two-step in the toy section.

In the afternoon, we drove back to the marina at Half
Moon Bay. We held hands as we stepped over the ropes and
onto the pier. Dozens of white fishing vessels had been out
during the early morning hours and had returned with their
catch. The bright sun reflected off the tubs of Dungeness
crabs, oysters, and fish that the fishermen
called out for us to buy. The pier gently
rocked with the waves; the smell of fish
filled the air. Seagulls circled in the blue sky,
and the breeze brought salt to our cheeks.

It is always moving
in us and through
us; it is always
inviting us home.

As we stood there together, I took all of it in: the ocean, the
sea life, the sky. There, with the love of my life, I felt the
wildness of the moment, the aliveness of it all. I remembered what I so often forget: that we are part of this creation. It is always moving in us and through us; it is always
inviting us home.

As we pulled into the driveway, kids poured out of the house.
After group hugs and kisses, we carried the Dungeness crabs
inside to prepare a feast. When we all sat together around the
big table, I smiled with a deep contentment.

Sometimes you need to go away in order to come home.

IV
Earth Lessons

I am well if you are well.

from a Shona greeting

There are trees in California—bristlecone pines—that were alive before the Great Pyramids were built in Egypt. There are olive trees in Israel that took root before Jesus walked the earth. In New Zealand, one kauri tree is twenty-one hundred years old and is believed to possess its own spirit. Some trees have a potential life span of nine thousand years. I am guessing that such trees possess great wisdom.

The tree that I sit by is not so ancient; however, she is one of my teachers. She grows beside a stream, and I cross a little bridge and walk down an embankment to get to her. The stream has washed away some of the soil around the tree, exposing the top of her wonderfully marbled roots. I sit on these roots with my questions, my longings, and my prayers, and I begin to feel grounded and rooted myself. I remember who I am, where I have come from, and where I'll return to. This tree contains the great cycle of the seasons in her being, and I witness the passage of time through her branches. My life is put into a much larger perspective, and I hear the invitation to align myself with the energy that animates this tree and all of this incredible creation.

As I sit under this tree, it makes perfect sense to me that the first place where Jesus was led after the Spirit came upon him in the Jordan was the wilderness. Nature is a great teacher; as Jesus lived among stones and trees and wild beasts, he learned from them, just as he was learning to listen to his own heart. His imagination was let loose among the wild things, and he returned with parables about mustard seeds and birds and trees, with stories of rains and winds and lilies of the field. He clearly saw the reign of God spread out upon the earth, and he used these images to help his followers see it as well.

When I sit on the roots of "my" tree, I have a sense of being home, of being connected to the life around me. I think of the words of many spiritual teachers who have described this deep interconnectedness. Teilhard de Chardin, Jesuit priest and scientist, wrote: "We are all of us together carried in the one world-womb." Black Elk prayed: "Great Spirit, Great Spirit, my Grandfather, all over the earth the faces of living things are all alike." And Chan K'in Viejo, a Lacandón spiritual leader, said: "What the people of the city do not realize is that the roots of all living things are tied together." Even some physicists are sounding like mystics these days, hypothesizing about "invisible fields" in which we all live and move and have our being.

If we are so deeply connected to one another and to our earth, then what we do individually affects the whole. We cannot continue to see ourselves as isolated individuals or to think that the choices we make have no impact on the world around us. Our roots are connected. The Shona people in Africa know this, and the manner in which they welcome one another reflects this sense of connection. It is a three-part greeting: "Good afternoon. How are you?" one person says. "I am well if you are well," says the other person. Upon hearing this, the first person says, "I am well, so we are well." In our one world-womb, I am truly well *only* if all other beings are well too.

Sometimes, when I look around at what we're doing to our earth, I feel overwhelmed. As a mother, I want my grandchildren and great-grandchildren to be able to sit by clear streams and learn from ancient trees. And so I go into the wilderness to listen to what the trees can teach me about strength and patience. I go to listen to my own heart as well, to try to understand what it is that I've been given to do. I think of cycles and seasons, of generations to come, of the legacies that we are passing on. I stand like a tree, in a stance that is open, receptive, and rooted. I stretch out my arms like branches, offering myself in service, releasing my prayer into the breeze: "May we *all* be well."

In our one world-womb, I am truly well *only* if all other beings are well too.

Porch Prayer

(WHILE GETTING THE MORNING PAPER)

I step out onto my porch and into this day that is now beginning. I greet the silent early dawn, and I am, once again, amazed.

The world beyond the door is a world of green and a world of light. Its beauty stuns me. The sunlight is beginning to dissipate the darkness. In the stillness, it happens slowly, almost imperceptibly. The world is coming alive once again. Shafts of light break through branches and inflame the grasses while the leaves on the trees shimmer with praise. Brown squirrels, with wild leaps of recognition that a new day is born, jump from the fence to the elms. Ants climb with the sun, white flies take their place in space, spiders crawl out of the gaps. We all begin to take up whatever it is we were born to do.

As I stand here, I hear the world of our ancestors, a world where rivers clap their hands with joy, and mountains and hills break into song. The *Alleluia!* is happening in our midst, and I want to bow down in full prostration, leap in circles of praise, join in the dance of incarnation that is happening this morning on my own front lawn.

My body responds in ways beyond conscious thought; I feel the energy of the morning taking effect in my cells. It is as if my body is singing a response to the earth's song, delighting in this homecoming. There is an attunement, that restoration of soul that the psalmist knows happens only in green pastures.

All of it becomes my offering: "Blessed are you, Awesome One; through your goodness we have this earth, this light, this green, this new day, to offer back to you. May it all become the gift of life. Blessed are you forever." I offer life back to the Creator, to the one whose presence lights up the trees and spiders and tiny grasses. And then, for just a moment, I catch a glimpse of the divine looking out through all of creation, and I gasp. The boundaries that normally separate us now disappear, and I experience the deep interconnectedness of all things.

The *Alleluia!* is happening in our midst, and I want to bow down in full prostration, leap in circles of praise, join in the dance of incarnation that is happening this morning on my own front lawn.

In parts of India, women paint their prayers on the ground outside their doors every morning. Taking rice flour or the powder of white stone, they draw *kolams*—magnificent patterns, unbroken lines of beauty—at the entrance of their homes and pray for blessings for their families. The women are the guardians of the threshold, of the liminal space between the spiritual and material worlds. From generation to generation, mothers teach their daughters how to greet the day.

Here on my porch, I paint my prayer with words. And I too try to teach my children how to greet the day. As each child wanders downstairs, I extend an invitation. "Come and see," I tell them.

Can you teach awe? Can you teach another how to catch a glimpse of God or how to hear trees clap and hills sing? Can you teach someone how to see burning bushes or parting seas or how to recognize holy ground when it is stumbled upon?

I do not know. I simply show my children what I see, then step back and let the wonder and marvel of an ordinary morning work its extraordinary miracle in their hearts.

Night

Debbie's aging mother has gone downhill fast. It has taken Debbie by surprise. She doesn't know how to be a parent to her mom; she has to reach inside herself to unfamiliar places and attempt to bring up resources she doesn't know she'll find.

This morning, I take advantage of a break in the rain and head out for a walk. At the end of my driveway, I see Debbie walking her new dog. We live next door to each other, yet in our busy lives we rarely say more than a quick hello. Today, I let go of my going-for-a-walk agenda and stop to talk. She introduces me to her dog, a nine-year-old gray terrier whose former owners had to tearfully give her away because their little granddaughter had come to live with them. I pat the dog, and we chat about leashes, laptops, and life. Then Debbie hints that the last few months with her mother have been very difficult.

"What's been the hardest part for you?" I ask.

Her eyes well up with tears. "The middle of the night. Getting up at three in the morning to change Mom's diapers and having her look me in the eyes and ask, 'Where's Debbie?'"

I don't know what to say. Then I remember a passage from a wonderful little book that I read yesterday. In it, the author, Jane Ellen Mauldin, recounts a wakeful night with her son, a night in which he kept calling out for her, a night in which she felt exhausted, grumpy, and alone. What got her through it was recalling a truth:

> **As I trudged alone through the night hallways, I staggered to a call as old as humankind. That night and every night, mothers and fathers around the world awaken to reassure restless children. That night and every night, grown children arise to calm fitful, aging parents. Those night hours are long and lonely. Our burdens and tired bones are ours alone to bear. There are, however, other people out there who are waking even as we are. There are other people who bear similar burdens—whether it is simply to reassure a child for one night, or to help a dying loved one be at peace, week after week, until the end.**
>
> **We who rise do so because we choose to do it. It is an intense, physical demand; it is also an honor as ancient as human love. We are part of the circle of families and friends who nurture Life, from its earthly beginning until its earthly conclusion.**

I share what I can remember of this with Debbie, and her eyes tear up. I tell her to call me if she ever needs anything during those midnight hours, that I too am likely to be awake, but with the other end of the life cycle—with my young daughter, who comes nightly into our bedroom and stands beside us until we wake and let her into the coziness of our bed.

All that separates our two houses are a few walls, a walkway, and seventy-three years between the two people who need us. To care for them *is* an honor as ancient as love.

Generations

I am a daughter. I am in kindergarten. My grandmother is asleep on the couch, wrapped in a crocheted coverlet that is her cocoon. She is always resting on the couch, except when she sits up to tell us to wear our sweaters on hot summer days. She will not emerge from this chrysalis state for a few more years. My mother is always mad at her for complaining about her sore feet and then refusing to go shopping for new shoes. My grandmother says her feet hurt too much to go out. My mother thinks she is exaggerating the pain and keeps bringing home new black laced shoes for her to try on. None are good enough.

My younger brother is teasing my two girl cousins, ages three and five. They are living with us for a while because their parents are getting a divorce. My younger sister plays with her dolls. We have a picture of her sitting on her bed with thirty dolls lined up beside her, and it is hard to tell which one is the real girl. My mother is pregnant with her fourth child in five years. My father is working two jobs. The eight of us live in a tiny house. I am happy.

I am learning valuable lessons. I discover that love can squeeze into tight places and that when there's a need, there's always room for one more.

❖

I am a daughter taking on the role of mother. I am fourteen.
I am sitting by the living-room window on a stormy night;
it is three in the morning, and I am waiting for my parents
to come home. They have been at a party, and I know they
have been drinking heavily. Every time a car passes by, I
startle. I don't know how to make sense of the mix of fear
and rage that I feel. If they die, will I be left to raise my
younger brother and sisters? Do courts give custody to
fourteen-year-olds?

My mother and father are struggling with depression and
alcoholism. As the oldest child, I feel a great weight of
responsibility. I hate being the bad mother, the one who
yells at them when I discover that they've been drinking.
When I come home after school and find my mother passed
out on the bed, or when my dad calls and says he won't be
home until very late, I get so angry. But mostly I'm scared,
and I don't understand. If they really loved us, wouldn't
they stop?

It is such a change from my childhood. They took such
good care of us for so many years. My mom would take us
to classes at the park, hide our lunches for treasure hunts,
spend hours with us at the beach. My dad would take us on
vacations and play touch football with all the neighborhood
kids. What happened to change them?

During these teenage years, I learn that life brings ten
thousand joys and ten thousand sorrows. I develop keen
senses and a strong intuition. I master the ability to think

through worst-case scenarios in six seconds flat. I discover a hidden strength within me where God resides, and I never feel alone.

❖

I am a mother. I am twenty-five. As I bring my firstborn son home from the hospital, I realize that the Lamaze classes prepared me for birth, but not for life after birth. Carrying him out of the hospital, I cannot believe they're going to let me take him home. I don't know what I'm doing. When is the real mom going to show up?

We get home, and it's time to change his diaper. His stool is black and sticky, and I hope that's normal. My mother-in-law has given me a caseload of cloth diapers with safety pins. I've only practiced with disposable diapers, but I feel obligated to make use of her gift. I stick myself three times, and the diaper hangs loosely around Ben's skinny legs. The next time he wets, it leaks all over, and I have to change my clothes.

When I nurse him, the pain is excruciating. No one told me about this. I sit and cry, my nipples bleeding and my uterus cramping. Relatives insist I give him a bottle, but I am determined to nurse. I lock myself in my room with him, crying, nursing, rocking. I am in love with him, and I am more exhausted than I ever thought possible. Fluids are seeping from every orifice of my body. I want a mother.

In the midst of my deepest joy, I begin to grieve. More than at any other time in my life, I want a mother who can come and tell me about all this, who can teach me how to be a mother myself, who can reassure me that I'm doing so well.

But my mother is still in the difficult years. She and my father are still struggling with depression, and they are still drinking. They are also on the verge of separating and have little energy for anything else but their own problems.

During this time, I develop competence. I learn how to change diapers with one hand, nurse the baby in any and every location, and pack an entire household into a diaper bag. I discover, day by day, that I *am* the real mom. And I gradually let grief break open my heart. I begin to accept that my mother is just who she is and that she loved me the best she could.

I am a granddaughter. Both of my grandmothers have been dead for many years. I am pregnant with my fourth child. I know that I will have a girl. I invite my mother out for coffee because I've been thinking about female lineage, about what is passed down from each generation. I want to hear again the story of her mother.

My grandmother—Eileen—was a high school French teacher. She was beautiful and petite, an artist and a socialite. She had studied one summer at the Sorbonne and had spent the rest of her life telling everyone about those days. My great-grandmother spoiled her daughter, making Eileen's clothes, dressing her as if she were a doll. She did this until Eileen finally left home at age forty to marry. My grandfather, a simple Irishman who was charming and gregarious, owned a grocery store and extended so much credit to his customers that he was never successful in business. They immediately had two children: first my mother, then my uncle. That was when Eileen's body and spirit fell apart.

When she was giving birth to her son, something went wrong. She developed an embolus that went into her pituitary artery, causing adrenal deficiencies and hypothyroidism. From that point on, she was sluggish and spent most days in bed. At age three, my mother found herself responsible for her little brother.

As my mother recounts those times, she speaks about the fear she felt as she sat at her living-room window, waiting for my grandmother to return from a rare trip to the city. She was terrified that her mother would die in the snowstorm, and she would be left to raise her brother.

Eileen's dream was that her daughter would study French and music. My mother wanted to play. My grandmother did not understand her daughter's extroverted personality. When my mother was in ninth grade, my grandparents decided to move to California to be with other family members. The move devastated my mother, who was very popular in the same high school at which my grandmother had once taught. They moved to a tiny trailer park outside of Los Angeles. My grandmother spent her days in bed, and my mother was embarrassed to have any friends over. The laundry was left in piles all over the furniture, and the dishes were never done.

My mother did the cooking and cleaning, but she resented it, wanting only to be out with her friends.

My mother went to nursing school because she could afford it and live away from home. Shortly after graduating, she married my father. They had hoped not to get pregnant right away, even setting the wedding date so that the rhythm method would work and they could honeymoon without worry. My dad had counted on my mother's training as a nurse to get this right. Nine months and three days later, I was born.

Then my grandfather developed throat cancer, and so when I was a year old my grandparents came to live with us in a tiny house. My father took a third job to pay all the bills. My brother was born six months later. Then my grandfather died. Eileen lived with us off and on, until one day the doctors correctly diagnosed the cause of her quarter-of-a-century-long lethargy. They prescribed medication, and almost immediately she broke through her cocoon and rose off the couch and came alive. She moved into a retirement community and once again became the belle of the ball.

I feel sad as I hear the story. So many dreams deferred or left unrealized. But I also recognize that it was out of the pain of her life that my mother developed many of her strengths—her sense of humor, her ability to think through worst-case scenarios in six seconds flat, her creative flair for making things seem together (when in reality they were held together by Scotch tape), her willingness to care for others. I remember that we are all making it up as we go along, doing the best we can with whatever we've got.

> I remember that we are all making it up as we go along, doing the best we can with whatever we've got.

I am a mother. My daughter is in kindergarten. I am on my way to see my mother and to help her organize her apartment.

My mother's body is falling apart. Heart problems, breast cancer, and osteoporosis have all taken their toll. The bones in her right foot are deteriorating, and her hipbones are so thin that the doctors cannot take any bone from them to rebuild her foot. She complains about the pain and is always searching for shoes that will help. Her mother had osteoporosis, and in the end, a broken hip probably eventuated in her death. My mother is stumbling more and more.

I pick up a box stuffed with receipts, dollar bills, medicine bottles, and old photos and ask her where I should begin. She looks at me, her eyes filling up with tears.

"I'm so overwhelmed." Her voice breaks. "I remember going through my mother's things and throwing away so much against her will." Now she is sobbing.

My heart opens, and for the first time in a long while I feel no need to defend against her. I put down the box and go over to her, putting my arms around her shrinking body. She feels so fragile and vulnerable.

"I have so much guilt about my mother," she stammers. I have a hard time making out her words because she is crying so hard. "I was so mean to her about her shoes. I didn't understand."

I clasp her head against my shoulder. "It's okay, Mom. It's all okay."

I give her a long hug. We are both mothers and we are both daughters. We have suffered, and we have loved the best we could. Right now I am grateful to be standing here with her, both of us tearful, holding each other tight—aware of a grace that has always been with us, weaving through it all.

Blessing One Another

The bud
stands for all things,
even for those things that don't flower,
for everything flowers, from within, of
    self-blessing;
though sometimes it is necessary
to reteach a thing its loveliness,
to put a hand on its brow
of the flower
and retell it in words and in touch
it is lovely
until it flowers again from within, of
    self-blessing.

Galway Kinnell

I thought I was going shopping to get out of the heat. I didn't know that I was going in order to offer a blessing and to be blessed in return.

It was a very hot day. In search of air conditioning, I took Julianna to a nearby shopping mall. I put her in her stroller, and we walked past all the display windows, stopping here and there. We ended up going into a discount department store, not looking for anything in particular.

As we turned into the toy aisle, we saw a young girl of seven or eight. We watched as she went to a shelf and carefully picked up a long stick with a beautiful cloth butterfly attached to one end. She held it high in the air; then, with absolute delight, she began to dance. She twirled around and around, yellow and pink and purple streamers flowing down around her in rivulets of color. Sparkles of light reflected off the tiny rhinestones on the butterfly wings, mixing together with the sparkle in the girl's eyes. It was as if we had turned the corner and entered Oz—only this was much more real. Julianna and I were mesmerized. What a thing of beauty—to witness all of this aliveness right here in this otherwise drab and cluttered aisle. We were totally caught up in this moment, swept up into this girl's imagination, which was allowing her to be a butterfly, utterly free and able to soar to great heights.

"What do you think you're doing?!" A sharp voice broke our trance. A tall, angry woman with blond hair pulled tightly into a bun rushed over to the child. Her badge identified her as an assistant manager of the store.

"Have you paid for that?" she shouted. "You have to buy that first if you're going to hold it!"

The dance stopped. The colors disappeared. The little girl stood immobilized, and the butterfly fell to the floor. Lovely brown eyes searched in panic for a mother's face.

Immediately her mother, who had been looking at dresses for her daughter, heard the commotion and hurried over. "What did you say?" she demanded of the manager, seeing the fear on her little girl's face.

"Is this your child?" the blond woman asked testily.

"Yes, she is. What is the problem?" the mother asked.

"You cannot play with toys unless you have purchased them. It looks like she's just taking it. Pay for it or put it back," the woman directed angrily.

I understood immediately what was happening. If Julianna had been the one dancing with the butterfly, there would have been no such scene. But this little girl did not look like someone this assistant manager wanted in the store. This child's skin was too dark; her kind was not to be trusted. This woman had to guard against such people, and it infuriated her that their numbers were growing by the day. Soon they would take all of the toys; they would take everything.

The girl's mother also knew what was happening. She had faced the same accusations herself, probably many times, in direct and not so direct ways. She pulled her daughter next to her, pushing her cart in order to move away. The assistant manager pursued them, and I heard shouts in Spanish and English coming from several aisles over. Then I heard the mother call out for the girl's grandmother, who apparently

had been looking at purses in a different department. Soon
all of the women were yelling as they moved around the
store, the little girl in tow.

I pushed Julianna's stroller down the candle aisle, my stomach
in knots. I am not the bravest person in the world. I am often
afraid of interfering, worried that my involvement might
seem intrusive. And some of the world's indifference has
rubbed off on me. But something happened to me in that
moment. I thought of the little girl's face and of the butterfly
crumpled on the floor. A deep and fierce energy began to stir
in me. I had a little epiphany in the aisle. I could not ignore
what was happening just because it was not happening to
"my child." I realized that she *was* my child, and whether the
assistant manager liked it or not, this girl was *her* child as
well. She had forgotten this, and she had forgotten her own
loveliness. I forget this too. I get all tied up in knots of fear
and doubt, and I can't move. It's a lonely place. But as I
pushed my daughter in her stroller, I began to remember
something different, and I knew I had to act.

The mother and grandmother and little girl made their way
to the front counter. The girl was now sobbing. "Please, I
want to speak with the manager," the mother said to an
employee as she stroked her daughter's head. "That woman
is verbally attacking my daughter." The employee called over
the loudspeaker for the manager, and the assistant manager
stormed away. I pushed the stroller over to the counter.

"I saw what happened, and I'll be happy to tell the manager,"
I offered. The mother looked at me with surprise; she did
not expect that someone would come forward and support

them. "Did you hear what she accused my daughter of?" she asked shakily. I told her I had, and then I spoke with the little girl, assuring her that she had done nothing wrong.

As we waited for the manager, I got a glimpse into this family's pain. The suffering caused by such prejudice, all too familiar to the grandmother and the mother, was now being passed on to yet another generation. Right before the mother's eyes, her daughter's birthright, the blessing of loveliness, was being stripped away. I felt a stab of sadness at the thought of this woman trying to protect her child, saying words of kindness in the hopes of restoring to the girl a sense of her goodness. But I also thought how different it would be if she had help. What if she had all of us doing this with her, reminding her daughter of her beauty? How different this girl's life would be.

The manager came over and asked what had happened. He listened with compassion to all of our accounts. He apologized, saying there was no excuse for the assistant manager's behavior and that she would be reprimanded and given sanctions.

The mother turned to me. "Thank you," she said quietly. "Gracias," said the grandmother. It made my heart hurt to see the little girl still trembling. I knelt down to touch her arm. "Bye, sweetheart," I said. She gave me a smile through her tears.

As I walked back into the shopping mall, a strange thing happened. I started seeing my children all over the place—climbing on benches, holding hands with their parents, sitting in strollers. I recognized them when I looked in their eyes. I began waving to them, and they waved back. And right then, I knew that this is how we help God out: by telling one another in words and in touch that we are lovely and whole and worthy of blessing. If we do our job, then one day the magic will happen. We will *all* blossom, every one of us. Together we will emerge like butterflies, soaring and dancing in sunlight, our hearts shimmering with praise.

The Wisdom of the Heart

Sharing many experiences of this sort with
people has made me wonder about the nature
of the heart. Perhaps the heart is not just a
sort of valentine. More than a way of loving,
the heart may be a way of experiencing life,
the capacity to know a fundamental connection
to others and see them whole.

Rachel Naomi Remen

Amelia Claire was born on the morning of November 23, 1995, during the Macy's Thanksgiving Day Parade. The actual moment of my niece's birth occurred as the Spiderman balloon floated by. This important fact has become part of our family story, and there is great hollering and hooting every year when that particular balloon comes into view on our television screen.

Amelia decided to make her appearance a few days early, interrupting our carefully laid out Thanksgiving dinner plans. She was a beautiful baby, with thick black hair that stuck straight up; she looked very different from her older sister, Christine, who has long blond ringlets. Amelia scored high on her Apgar ratings. The doctor mentioned, almost as an offhand remark, that she had heard a slight murmur in Amelia's heart and that her regular pediatrician should listen again at her two-week checkup. After one night at the hospital, the happy family went home.

On Friday, Paul and I and our two-month-old Julianna showed up at their door with a day-late but delicious Thanksgiving feast. We took turns holding Amelia; she was a very quiet baby, and she slept a lot. My sister Nancy was determined to breast-feed her. But Amelia didn't nurse for very long at any one time, and Nancy struggled not to blame herself when it seemed Amelia was losing weight.

Two weeks went by, and Amelia had her first checkup. The doctor was surprised to discover two ear infections—and a heart murmur that was significant enough to warrant a referral to a cardiologist. Over the next two days I did a little research, putting together symptoms I saw in Amelia with what the medical book described. I was horrified to discover that she exhibited all the signs of congestive heart failure. I encouraged Nancy to move the appointment time up, and she was able to take Amelia in the next day.

The cardiologist told Nancy and her husband, Mark, what he had found: Amelia had a large hole in her heart, in the wall between the ventricles. Her heart was pumping very inefficiently, which accounted for her sleepiness. There was fluid around her heart, and the doctor prescribed a diuretic. He said surgery might be needed, but he was hoping it could wait until she got bigger.

That day marked our family's entrance into another
world—the world of doctors' offices, hospitals, and med-
ications. Nancy describes it as stepping into a different
universe. She was going along one day, and everything
was wonderful; the next day, her life was turned upside
down. She had no idea how she was going to handle it.
She kept looking around, waiting for someone to arrive
and make everything right again or deal with everything
for her. When people asked her how she was, either she
numbly answered, "Fine," or she began spewing out, like
an expert, medical terminology that she hadn't known a
week before.

And yet, for all of us, it was also stepping into a place of
authenticity. When we come to the edge of life, we realize how
little control over it any of us really has. We discover what
really matters, and the priorities of one day become inconse-
quential the next. We know that holding one another close is
our most important task.

The next month was a mix of sleeplessness and fear as things
became even more difficult for Amelia. Nancy was asked to
stop breast-feeding, and Amelia began to throw up all of her
formula. She was losing weight, and at one month old, she
weighed less than she had at birth. A gastroenterologist
ordered medical tests. An inept technician attempted to do
heel sticks on her, but kept missing her veins, causing
Amelia, Nancy, and Mark to cry for an hour in the lab.
On Christmas Eve, we all sat under the tree, opening presents
and feigning cheerfulness, our hearts breaking every time
Amelia threw up or whimpered.

But in January, things began to improve. Amelia began to hold down her formula, and we held a party on the day she passed her birth weight, making it to eight pounds. There were hopes that as she grew, the hole in her heart would close on its own; however, these hopes were ended by the next visit with the cardiologist. He recommended that she undergo surgery at UCSF, performed by the doctor who had pioneered infant heart surgery. The hospital originally scheduled the operation on January 31, but when the doctor heard that that day was Amelia's sister's fourth birthday, he moved the surgery up by a week. None of us wanted to admit that he did so because he didn't want Christine's birthday to be forever haunted by Amelia's failure to come through the surgery.

Two nights before the surgery, we held a prayer service for Amelia. We touched our own hearts and then gently laid our hands on her heart. We prayed that the connection we felt with her would sustain her in surgery. We asked for strength for Nancy and Mark, that they would be able to hold their daughter close, let her go, and—we prayed— receive her back again.

The night before the surgery, Nancy and Mark took Amelia and checked into a small hotel in San Francisco. They bundled her up, walked up and down the foggy hills, and then came across a church. They went inside, and in the beautiful, silent darkness, they lit candles and prayed. Never before had they felt so in need of something, and their prayers reflected that.

The next morning, Paul and I and Julianna made the hour-long drive to San Francisco in order to pick them up and drive them to the hospital. We left at six o'clock, and as we drove, it was strange to see life continuing on as usual—people on their way to work, people walking their dogs, businesses getting ready for another day. We couldn't believe the surgery was really going to happen; there was a sense of unreality to the whole morning.

After Amelia and her parents got in our van, we drove to UCSF. We went inside, and Nancy and Mark went to talk with the surgeon, who is, statistically speaking, the best in the world at what he does. He was very reassuring to my sister, and he said that he has a sense that God is involved when he performs a surgery. "There are times when I do things that I should not be able to do," he said with great humility.

The surgeon went on to describe the procedure, comparing it to going through the top of a Christmas tree ornament with delicate instruments in order to sew up a hole in the middle. At two months old, Amelia's heart was a very tiny thing. It was the size of her fist and weighed only two-thirds of an ounce.

We all had a chance to touch little Amelia, who was barefoot and smiling in her hospital gown, and give her a blessing and a kiss. Nancy and Mark were anxious to get the surgery over with, but were reluctant to let their baby go. They took another minute with her, memorizing everything about her. Finally they said good-bye.

Then the wait began. We wiped away tears, read books, went in shifts to the cafeteria, made phone calls. And we began to witness other stories. One young couple was waiting for their year-old son to come out of eye surgery. The doctor came in, and we overheard his quiet news.

"I'm very sorry, but we weren't able to correct the problem."

"Does that mean he'll be blind for life?"

"I'm sorry. Yes, it does."

The woman choked back a sob, and the husband set down the materials on Braille that he had been reading so that he could hold his wife.

Other stories broke open our hearts. One two-year-old had been born with no small intestine and was undergoing her fifth surgery. Another baby, this one a twin, had been born with a severe heart defect. He survived surgery, but now there were complications.

We met parents who are absolute heroes, saints whose daily acts of love and bravery are beyond comprehension. Suddenly, we began to feel lucky—or even a tiny bit guilty—that Amelia had "only" a hole in her heart.

After many hours, Nancy and Mark were called in to talk with the doctor. "Things went well," he said. Those were the most important words they had ever heard. He went on to describe the surgery. Amelia had had one big hole that had been patched with some of her own heart tissue, and she had had a few smaller holes as well, which had been stitched closed. The doctor had wrapped a wire around her sternum to hold it together; as she grows, cartilage will grow over it. Finally able to smile, Nancy jokingly asked if Amelia would now set off all the airport metal detectors with her internal wire.

There were tears of relief and great rejoicing, and we held a pizza party in one of the lounges. And yet as we celebrated, we were always conscious of those parents in the other room who were waiting for the news of their own children. Eventually we were able to take turns seeing Amelia in the ICU. She was covered with tubes and wires, and the incision on her chest went from her throat to her mid-abdomen. And yet she was absolutely beautiful. A nurse had taken a white ribbon with red hearts and had made a bow around her black hair.

I spent the night at the hospital with Nancy, and Paul took Julianna home. I was still nursing at the time, and it was an uncomfortable night without my baby nearby. I wanted so much to hold her; I've never felt more grateful.

Early the next morning, Nancy and I went in to visit Amelia. We couldn't hold her, but we loved just being in her presence. And then suddenly, while we were in with her, the alarms on the machines started to go off. We looked at each other, and a nurse called for assistance.

Nancy and I backed up against a wall and held each other's hands. Amelia's heart had started to experience tachycardia and was beating about three hundred times a minute. We froze, filled with absolute terror as more and more medical personnel were called in. They kept giving her drugs, saying, "Push—STAT." Her heart would calm down, and then it would begin to race again. It felt as if our own heart rates matched hers.

A doctor finally noticed us and yelled, "Get the mother out of here!" We were ushered out, left to pace in agony in the waiting room. After an interminable amount of time, we went back in to ask what was happening. We were told that Amelia was going to be fine. The surgery had irritated the electrical impulse of her heart, but the drugs had been able to stabilize her again.

After that scare, things went well. Several more days passed, and finally we were allowed to bring Amelia home. Nancy and Mark said good-bye to the other parents that they had met. They heard that the twin boy who had experienced complications from heart surgery had died the night before. The girl who had had intestinal surgery had an infection and might require another surgery. As they stood in the elevator, they met a woman who was eight months pregnant; she was on her way to the pediatric cancer ward, where her two-year-old had just been diagnosed with liver cancer.

Nancy and Mark were the ones, on that morning, who were bringing home a healthy baby, one who would grow stronger each day. Not a lot of this made sense to them. The only thing that made any sense was their deep realization of the holiness and value of each and every life.

Amelia's heart was not the only heart that grew stronger through this experience. We all experienced a healing of our hearts as we discovered a fundamental truth: We are all connected to one another, by our heartbeats and by our love.

The Mother's Journey

I have hands big enough
to save the world,
and small enough
to rock a child to sleep.

Zelma Brown

Looking up at the night sky is a humbling experience. The great darkness invites us to think about where we fit in, where we stand between the past and the future, between the earth and the stars. We seek to understand who we are and what it is that we are supposed to do.

One warm summer night, when I was very pregnant with Julianna, I went outside to sit in a pool of cool water under the stars. I slowly massaged my growing belly, imagining who this child would be and what she would bring into this universe. As I looked up at the light from the stars, light that has taken millions of years to reach us, I thought about ancestors. If only one great-great-grandparent had been a different person, I would not be here, and I would not be pregnant with this unique soul.

On that night, I also thought of the future ones yet to be born. I knew that my daughter was already fully formed, that in her ovaries were all the thousands of eggs she would ever carry. In that moment under the stars, I realized that I was carrying within me the seeds of my grandchildren, who would be alive into the twenty-second century.

Suddenly, the distance between centuries did not seem so great. I felt myself participating in a much larger story. I understood that as a mother, I am part of a long continuum, carrying in my being both my ancestors and the future generations. With that comes the kind of responsibility that Native American wisdom articulates: "In our every deliberation, we must consider the impact of our decisions on the next seven generations." What I do here and now will affect many more lives than my own.

It's easy to lose sight of this larger perspective when we're caught up in daily life—signing permission slips, making lunches, teaching our children to be kind to one another. It doesn't feel as if we're doing anything truly profound. And yet with each kiss, with each lesson, we are doing the work of the ages. We are nurturing life, we are shaping the next generation's hearts and bodies and souls.

Literature is full of stories about the hero's journey. More often than not, these stories are about men, about how they go forth and slay the dragon or save the town, bringing back the Holy Grail or a gift for the community. There are fewer examples of women as heroes. Perhaps we need to rethink the idea of what an adventurous life is, of what a heroic journey entails. It might involve a quest, or it might be that we do not have to go anywhere else to obtain the gift, because we already hold it in our hands. We bring life to the community through our children and our work.

Perhaps we need to rethink the idea of what an adventurous life is, of what a heroic journey entails.

Standing under the night sky, I ask the ancestors, the great communion of saints, to be with us on our journey. I ask them for wisdom and courage and strength to do the work that must be done. I reach out across time and ask the future ones, those waiting to be born, for their prayers and their trust that we will act like ancestors and pay attention to the longer rhythms of life.

With hands big enough to save the world and small enough to rock our children to sleep, we pray for the grace to fulfill our quest.

Holy Ground

I have walked on this earth for more than four decades. Most of my steps have been taken in forgetfulness; a few have been taken with some degree of awareness. When I am awake enough to know that I am walking on holy ground, something shifts inside of me. I take in the earth's wisdom, and it helps me move more deeply into my own life.

It's been said that angels whisper to you when you go for a walk. Maybe that's why walking meditation is such a powerful way to pray. After walking, I often record my reflections in my journal. I'll share a few of these with you now. I invite you to read them slowly, to picture the scenes, and to listen for the angels' whisper in your own ears as you accompany me on these walks.

I .
(When I was nineteen, I attended a writers' conference held in the countryside of northern California. During a lunch break, we were invited to go for a walk to a nearby waterfall, and I jotted down these reflections.)

The yellow letters on the sign spell out PRAYER CHAPEL
and the arrow points to the left.
I smile.
I, too, am going to a prayer chapel.
I turn to the right and walk to the Falls.

There is a time for speaking
and a time to keep so quiet
that you can hear wings touch the grass.
Some people choose to speak.
Their thoughts carry them along at breakneck speed;
they even miss the trees.
A narrow dirt path becomes a freeway.

A huge white turtle, its neck extended,
moves slowly across the sky.
I look down for a moment to see where I am going.
When I look back up, the turtle has changed itself
into a powerful elephant.
I love surprises.

"It's time for a picnic!" the lush green grasses call out
   to me.
"Not now. Perhaps later," I tell them.
But I know that if I don't go now, I never will.

A fallen log makes believe that it's a huge metal pipe.
A rusted metal pipe pretends to be a log.
They both chuckle to themselves.
The people sitting on them
don't even know the difference.

The green moss-covered rocks brace themselves,
giant frogs trying to hold back the stream.
The water pays them no heed
and flows over their slimy backs.

The sound of my footsteps on this rocky path
makes more noise
than the distant waterfall.

Quietly, in the shadows,
pale green lichen blooms
in miniature petals—
its gift to the rock.

Black jeweled dragonflies
hang like notes in the air,

the music of the Falls.
I fly from the dry land
to kiss the water with them,
and move in their symphony.
When I leave this place,
dragonflies follow.

(After this walk, we returned to class to do another writing exercise, and I wrote down, for the very first time, my feelings about my parents' alcoholism. I let out the family secret. Perhaps the walk provided me with a sense of safety, and I knew at a deep level that it was time to begin my own healing process.)

I I .

(I wrote this journal entry many years later, when I was the mother of three boys, ages six, eight, and ten. I had just attended a workshop that was entitled "Water from the Rock: Tapping the Deep Sources." The timing of the workshop was particularly meaningful, because it came at the end of a long California drought. The focus was on finding one's creative self and on moving from a time of inner drought to one of breakthrough. During the workshop, I realized that I needed to break free of some old patterns; I knew that I had to leave my present job and take the risk of following my dreams. As I was returning home, it began to rain for the first time in five years.)

It has been so long since the storms. As I drive home today, the rain pours down hard and wonderful on my windshield. I feel a release; I'm alive again and in love with the world.

I've been living such a controlled life, one that makes sure I never get wet. At a stoplight, I realize that my children don't even remember rain; the drought has been going on for so many years . . . it's been going on in so many ways. I know what I must do when I return home.

"Who wants to go for a walk?" I ask upon opening the door. Paul looks at me as if I've lost my mind. "No umbrellas allowed," I add. They all accept my invitation.

My children have never seen their mother like this, but they're happy to go outside. The five of us walk down the street, delighting in getting wet. We take a detour in order to watch a rushing creek pouring over what has been for many years merely a parched bed. The boys watch wide-eyed. Matthew was still breast-feeding when the rains last came; he has never seen water fall from the sky.

The boys discover deep puddles, jumping in with both feet. I don't worry about shrinking shoes—better their shoes than their spirits. At first, Paul has a harder time than I do with letting go, with not calling out, "Stay out of the puddles." But then a car drives by and the four people inside of it stare at us, curious about what these strange people are doing out in the rain. Paul sees us with new eyes and waves at the car. Then he and the boys have a water fight, kicking water from puddles in order to drench one another.

When we arrive home, we take off our shoes and jackets, and I go to start a bubble bath for the boys. Paul makes a fire and hot cocoa, and soon we are all bundled up on the couch, talking about our walk. The boys ask if we can do it again tomorrow.

I have not felt this alive in a long, long while. The long drought is over.

I I I .
(I wrote this entry last year. I had not been feeling very creative. I doubted myself; I doubted that I had anything much to offer; I doubted that the universe would provide. I went and sat in my van near a local apricot orchard. It was almost spring, and the ground beneath the newly budding trees was blanketed in wild mustard plants—acres of yellow flowers for as far as the eye could see. I decided to walk around the perimeter of the orchard; I returned amazed and filled with faith.)

This morning, millions and millions of yellow petals are ablaze, lit from above and lit from within. The orchard is wholly fire; the flowers beckon me like some burning bush. "Pay attention," they sing. "Behold the miracle," they call.

I go out to meet them in spite of myself.

The walk begins quietly enough. The mustard plants grow beside the path, giving me some distance from their energy. But around the bend, the path disappears as the plants close ranks. Suddenly I find myself stepping, chest-deep, into an ocean of yellow waves. "Launch into the deep and you shall see," said Jacques Ellul, and I wonder for a moment if I dare. But it is too late to turn around; I am surrounded, and I take the plunge. Wet petals cling to my arms and my legs;

when I look down, I can no longer see my shoes. When I look up, there is brilliance in every direction. I am standing, openmouthed, in extravagance.

When Jesus talked about mustard seeds, he said outlandish things like "This is what the kingdom of heaven is like" and "Nothing will be impossible to you." He talked about moving mountains, about uprooting trees and planting them in the sea. As I stand in this field of unfurling grace, I understand. Nothing seems far-fetched when you're walking on water of gold.

I return, dazed, to my car. I sit and remove my wet walking shoes, noticing that tiny yellow petals have come with me. They cling to my shoes' white leather, and I let them stay where they are, happy to take them along as a reminder of possibilities.

And then I pick up my journal off of the car seat to write these reflections. As I open the pages, I read a passage from Annie Dillard's *Pilgrim at Tinker Creek* that I copied down just yesterday:

> **Martin Buber quotes an old Hasid master who said, "When you walk across the fields with your mind pure and holy, then from all the stones, and all growing things, and all animals, the sparks of their soul come out and cling to you, and then they are purified and become a holy fire in you."**

I get out of the van with my shoes removed, step onto the soft and holy earth, and bow.

V
Life Lessons

I Don't Know

from a sign in my office

In my therapy office, I have a small sign that sits on top of my rolltop desk. It has three simple words engraved in white letters on a wood-grain background. It reads: "I Don't Know." Sometimes clients ask me about this sign. A few are troubled by it, wanting a therapist who knows exactly what it is they should do with their lives. Others smile when they see it, and their bodies relax into their chair as they realize that it is all right to not have all the answers.

In my office, I have discovered that moving into the place of not knowing is exactly the place to begin. I sit with people—with couples who feel that a huge and unbridgeable gap has opened up between them, with individuals who feel such a gap existing within themselves, with families whose pain leaves them wounded and exhausted, with children who are frightened of the dark or of their parents' divorce. I listen to stories—of the young woman who no longer wants to live, of the nun who cuts herself to dull the pain of childhood abuse, of the man who lives in terror of his father. As I sit and listen and witness such suffering, I inevitably come to the place of not knowing.

Over the years, I have learned not to be afraid of this place. I enter it with a prayer, asking for guidance. And then I listen not only to the person in front of me, but also to my heart and to my body, listening for where the Spirit moves, for that place of fullness that exists just behind the emptiness. I let go of my own ideas and watch for the appearance of a thread, a thread that we can follow together. As we follow this thread, the person lets go and trusts the healing process as it moves through him or her. I am always amazed by this. At the very point of this person's greatest suffering, he or she uncovers an inner wisdom and compassion.

When I am not in my office, I sometimes forget that I don't know. I can become stuck in my habitual ways of seeing my children and friends and husband, not really open to seeing who they are in each moment. I forget to put on Beginner's Mind and instead act as if I have all the answers. It is often hard for me to simply wait and trust the process.

In my office, I have discovered that moving into the place of not knowing is exactly the place to begin.

But the truth is that I don't know. I don't know how it is that days filled with children and noise and mess and clutter can seem endless, and then, when the kids are grown, it can seem as if those same days passed ever too quickly. I don't know how many billions of stars are up in the sky or how suffering can hold the seeds of resurrection. I don't know how to answer all my children's questions, or my own. I don't know how to completely let go.

Life keeps inviting me to learn these things, presenting me each and every day with opportunities for growth. And it does seem that when I open my eyes and heart to others, I begin to recognize something that has been there all along. It feels like a presence, a light, a love, that is unbounded by time or space or matter. It moves within us and among us, healing us, filling us, calling us to recognize that what we seek is right here in our midst.

On my desk, beside my little "I Don't Know" sign, is a white orchid growing in a container. The white petals of three flowers have fallen off, and a new shoot has grown out of the old. There are six tiny buds along this new shoot, and they are growing toward the light. Every time I move the plant, they turn, aligning themselves with the sun's light streaming through the window. It is a simple, elegant act. In their natural wisdom, these blossoms know that being in alignment with this source of life is all they need to do. They trust this process, and the result is one of stunning beauty.

Hiding Places

My daughter, Julianna, has a favorite hiding place where she keeps things that she doesn't want the rest of us to find. It is an antique music cabinet made of marbled wood. It has an inset beveled mirror on top, and inside are six shelves for sheets of music. On the door is a tiny metal handle with a latch that, when it is opened, makes a little clicking sound. On any given day, one might find a dried leaf, or a Band-Aid, or a peanut butter cracker hidden away on its shelves.

This cabinet came to my mind today as I listened to a radio talk show on the topic of miscarriage. Many women, the commentator noted, never reveal their secret or talk about their grief. In many cases, the pregnancy does not yet show; because few people know these women were expecting, their loss remains hidden as well. Compounding their sense of isolation is the fact that in our society, we don't talk much about death. We hide it away, and we don't want to think about it.

Many women take their pain, their grief, their guilt and move it inside, into a private place where it is concealed from others and perhaps even from themselves. They try to figure out the cause of their loss and second-guess their every action. They torture themselves with secret thoughts such as *I shouldn't have had that glass of wine*, or *I should have taken vitamins,* or *There's something wrong with me; I'm being punished.*

One woman called in to the radio program and told the story of her own miscarriage. Shortly after she lost the baby, she spoke to her mother about it, and her mother said that she had never known a woman who had had a miscarriage. The young woman then told her grandmother, who lived in a nursing home. Her grandmother said that *she* had never known anyone who had miscarried. Wondering if her experience was really so unique, this young woman began to ask the other elderly women in the nursing home whether they had ever known anyone who had lost a pregnancy.

One by one, the stories emerged. These elderly women, some of whom had held in their secret for fifty or sixty years, began to cry as they remembered and gave voice to their pain. No one had ever asked them before now; no one had ever brought up this subject. Doors were opening, and the secret hiding places were being revealed.

On the same radio show, another woman called in and shared her story. She had experienced one miscarriage and then three failed IVF treatments, with the eventual loss of nine embryos. As part of her grieving process, she went out and gathered nine polished stones, carefully selecting each one. During her meditations, she spends time with each stone, holding them one by one in the palm of her hand. Eventually, when the time feels right, she will let them go, setting them into a nearby stream.

A third woman spoke of looking at herself in the mirror the night after a miscarriage, searching her reflection for the rest of her. In utter agony, she ran her hand over her swollen abdomen, wanting her baby to somehow come back. She realized that she was forever changed: she had lost not only the baby, but her trust in life as well.

As I listened to these stories, my own secret place was opened once again. I am always surprised at how close the tears can be, at how they can well up so quickly. Eight years ago, when I was nine weeks pregnant, Paul and I saw a strong heartbeat on the ultrasound machine. What we did not know was that the next day the little heartbeat would stop. However, my body did not seem to want to let go of this child, and I never had, as they say, a "spontaneous abortion." So I did not discover the miscarriage until my thirteenth week.

The day the Persian Gulf War began, I had a D&C. My memory of my recovery is of lying dazed on our couch, watching the television images of antiaircraft fire over Baghdad. Waves of grief washed over me as our loss blended with the death that was occurring on the other side of the world.

As my grief continued for many days, weeks, and months, so did my body's healing. I developed several infections and was often in physical pain. In my journal more than two months later, I wrote:

> I was unable to control (or was I?) the ending.
> And it doesn't end . . . it goes on, like the war, for seven weeks,

and even beyond the declaration of a cease-fire.
How can my body's healing take longer than a war?

Later that year, I became pregnant once again. My confidence
had been shattered, and for weeks I feared the telltale spot-
ting. And then, one morning when I was ten weeks pregnant
and just after we had again seen a strong heartbeat, I had a
second miscarriage. The cause remains a mystery.

For three years after that, I was unable to conceive. And then,
suddenly, I was pregnant. Once again, I had a miscarriage.
This one came earlier, at six weeks. At that point, Paul and I
let go of our dream of having a child together.

But life continues to bring the unexpected. After several
months, we were surprised by yet another pregnancy, this
one conceived on Christmas Eve morning. After nine
months of worry and prayer and grasping onto every shred
of hope I could, Julianna Noelle came into our world.

My experience of miscarriage and my experience of sitting
with people in therapy sessions have taught me that trying
to protect ourselves from pain by hiding it away does not
lead to healing. We might be afraid that our grief or anger
or pain will overwhelm us if we open the door. But locking
our pain away only deepens our sense of isolation; we suffer
unseen and alone. It is only when we have the courage to
open the door to the hidden parts of our lives that our suffering can be transformed into wisdom and compassion.

We cannot do this by ourselves. We need to take one another's hands as we open doors and uncover our pain. Over the course of our lifetime, we take turns: sometimes we hold; sometimes we are held. The important thing is that we do this together. We grieve, we give comfort and support, we tell each other that we are not alone. Then gradually we realize that we are healing, we are coming out of hiding, and we are learning how to trust and love again.

It is only when we have the courage to open the door to the hidden parts of our lives that our suffering can be transformed into wisdom and compassion.

No Words

On our human journey, we sometimes enter places of heartbreak, silent places where simply no words bring comfort or understanding or relief from incalculable pain.

There are also occasions when we witness such heartbreak; it is in these moments that compassion can be born in us. This involves a willingness to carry the burden with others, to take on their suffering in the hope that somehow that will make a difference for the ones who suffer, and for ourselves.

At 4:05 on Christmas morning, sirens woke me. For five minutes they sounded, and then they were joined by another round, more trucks being called in. And then more. For almost thirty minutes the sirens sounded. I tried to estimate their distance, the way one does with lightning and thunder. My guess was that whatever was happening was at least five miles away, perhaps in the industrial section of the city. I was wrong. Later, as I read the news reports, it was easy to imagine what might have happened.

It was Christmas Eve. The family arrived home at nine o'clock from a celebration at a relative's house. The mother and father began the ritual of putting their excited children to bed. Cookies and milk and carrots were set next to the fireplace, which was nice and clean for Santa's visit. Finally, all of the children—ages three, seven, nine, and ten—had their pajamas on and teeth brushed, and each had been kissed goodnight and tucked into bed.

Mom and Dad could now wrap the presents from Santa, staying up until two in the morning to put on the last of the bows and tags. Finally, in the early morning hours, they themselves went to sleep.

Just before four o'clock, Mom woke up. She smelled smoke and woke her husband. They tried to go and wake their three oldest children, but were forced back by scorching heat. Mom grabbed their three-year-old son and ran outside to seek help. Dad tried to get the other children, but he never made it. He was struck by burning rafters and overcome with smoke. He was found just two feet from his nine-year-old son, who also died in the fire. The seven-year-old daughter died of smoke inhalation on the way to the hospital. The ten-year-old daughter was in intensive care.

Our own daughter was sleeping in that Christmas morning, and by eight o'clock, Paul and I were wide awake, waiting for Julianna to get up and see what Santa had brought. It was then that I remembered the sirens. I turned on the

TV, expecting to hear a report about a factory explosion or chemical fire. Instead, I heard this brief report: "In the early morning hours, a family home was destroyed by fire. The father and two children were killed; the mother and their three-year-old son escaped, along with their ten-year-old daughter, who is in the hospital in very critical condition."

I felt numb. But just then Julianna appeared. After a big Christmas hug, the three of us went downstairs, and for a few hours I tried to put the news story out of my mind. Later, I heard the name of the street where the family lived. It was about a mile from our home.

Two mornings later, I woke early and decided to take some quiet meditation time. I went downstairs, made some tea, wrapped myself in a blanket, and sat on the couch. I slowed my breath, feeling peaceful and grateful. Then the mother who had lost her family came to my mind. I knew where she must have been right then—in the hospital, at the bedside of her young daughter, who lay in a coma in extremely critical condition. She would be keeping vigil, without her husband to support her, needing to be strong for her daughter, without time to fully grieve the deaths of her husband and two children. And with a three-year-old son who needed her.

As I got in touch with all of this, I was overcome with grief. What she was going through was beyond anyone's worst nightmare. I sobbed, repeating over and over again, "How can she bear it?"

And then I knew that she would not be able to bear it alone. She would need prayers and support and love if she was to survive. My sense was that if I allowed myself to feel this sorrow, somehow it would help her. I remembered that the Hebrew word for compassion is *rahamin*, which has the same root word as the word for womb, *rehem*. As a mother, I knew my grief over the unimaginable was welling up from that deep place inside me. I sensed my connection with her; I also sensed that if people would let this pain break open their own hearts, maybe just a fraction of this woman's burden would be relieved, even though it would remain almost impossible to bear.

Four days after Christmas, the ten-year-old daughter died from the effects of carbon monoxide poisoning. She would join her father, her brother, and her sister, whose bodies lay in the mortuary, awaiting burial.

I do not know how this mother survives.

I do know that she credits her faith and the love that she's received from God, from family and friends, and even from strangers as the reason she can get up in the morning.

Perhaps this is all any of us have. Perhaps this is enough.

The Christmas story is a story about entering into the human journey, about taking it on from the inside, not as a dispassionate observer, but as one who chooses to bear another's sorrow and pain. When we make that choice, I have to believe that it does make a difference—for the ones who suffer, and for ourselves.

Are We There Yet?

This month, I've passed a milestone. I have lived in this house for seven and a half years, longer than I've lived in any other house. To get to the previous record, you have to go back more than thirty years, to the little house on 87th Place.

I moved into that house in the middle of first grade, and the seven years I lived there seemed like an eternity. I can still draw the floor plan and describe in detail the huge apricot tree that was our playhouse and the secret place under the hedge where we'd sneak into the neighbor's yard.

After I graduated from eighth grade, my father quit his job and decided to start his own business in another city. We sold the house and packed up to move. My mother wanted to save money, so she hired a discount moving company that she could pay by the hour. To help speed the process and cut hours off of the movers' time, she promised the neighborhood kids a McDonald's lunch if they'd come and help us drag all of our furniture and about two hundred boxes out to the front lawn. A crowd of boys and girls arrived, and we had great fun sitting on our couch out in the sun, sipping lemonade and waiting for the moving van to arrive. One car driving by even stopped, and two ladies, thinking this was a yard sale, inquired about the price of a lamp.

Well, the hours passed, but the movers never showed up. At five o'clock my mother came out. "Guess what?" she said enthusiastically. "The movers just called. They won't be here until tomorrow. So let's move everything back inside!" Fourteen kids rolled their eyes and groaned. Nine said they heard their mothers calling and disappeared. The rest of us were not so lucky and spent the evening undoing our move.

The next morning, my mom wanted us to repeat the process, but we were a day older and wiser, and we went on strike. Eventually, the movers showed up, and there was great fanfare as they carried the last of the boxes onto their truck. We walked through our empty house one final time, patting the walls as we said good-bye to each room. Then the four of us kids piled into the backseat of our old white Buick while my parents sat in the front, hemmed in by plants and a birdcage. We headed for our new life.

As we drove over the hill separating Los Angeles from the San Fernando Valley, the number one song, "Leaving on a Jet Plane" by Peter, Paul and Mary, played over the radio. My siblings and I knelt on the backseat, looking out the rear window as we sang along at the tops of our lungs. All our bags were packed, we were ready to go, and we had no idea when or if we'd be back again. We were sad to leave our friends, yet we were also excited about this new adventure my mother had promised.

When we finished singing, the four of us turned around. My little sister asked my parents, "Are we there yet?" Little did we know that they had no clue where they were going.

The house we moved into was a three-thousand-square-foot home in Tarzana, on a block where a real movie star lived. It had a large pool and a view of the entire valley. My parents sat by the pool on Sunday mornings, sipping champagne and eating steak and eggs. "This is the life," they'd say as they clinked glasses. But something was wrong with this picture. We were broke. My dad's new business was not going well, and he lost what little he had invested in the stock market. My mom thought the fact that we had no money and yet were living in this exclusive neighborhood made for a great story. I thought it made for a nervous stomach.

Starting ninth grade at a new school was difficult for me. I was an introvert, and it was hard for me to make friends. My dad tried to help by giving me two books: *PsychoCybernetics,* which suggests that you imagine yourself on a movie screen being the person you want to be, and *How to Win Friends and Influence People,* which advises you to always remember people's first names. So I'd spend hours envisioning myself as a chatty and skinny girl in bell-bottom pants, on a first-name basis with the entire freshman class. It didn't work.

We lived in Tarzana for five months. Then my dad decided he wasn't cut out for self-employment, and he took a job managing a cable television station near San Diego. So we packed up our things and migrated south.

We lived in the next house for six months. And the one after that for nine months. All in all, we moved eleven more times in the next five years, up and down the state of

California. Our traveling troupe consisted of my parents, four kids, two dogs, a Siamese cat, and a white mouse. We lived in small houses, large houses, and even a motel room for a month. I attended seven high schools.

When people hear how often we moved, they ask if my dad was in the military. I tell them no, that my parents were searching for what they wanted to be when they grew up and they dragged their four children along behind them. My dad was a marketing manager who longed to be a football coach, and my mother was a nurse who dreamed of being a TV talk-show host. In our naivete, we kids kept asking at each move, "Are we there yet?" hoping against hope that the answer would be yes. But my parents would not arrive for many, many years. During this time, they struggled with depression and alcoholism as they searched for their place in this world.

It's common wisdom that our wounds teach us our most valuable lessons. I gained many things from these moving years: the knowledge that home is not a building, but a group of people that I love; the habit of journaling, with God as my pen pal; a love of books, in which I found companions for my journey; an adaptability of spirit, with an understanding of the impermanence of all things; and the ability to pack up a house in less than two days.

Three decades later, I sit in a house that I have lived in longer than any other. It's nice to be able to plant a lemon tree and be around long enough to see several dozen lemons grow, or to plant bulbs in the winter and see them emerge in the spring. Yet, to me, home will always be more than just a building that we can buy and sell through a realtor.

When I was a teenager, I made my parents a large felt banner that had pictures of our many, many houses. At the bottom, I embroidered the words "Wherever we are together, we're home." That still sums it up for me. Home is where we are with those we love.

And the funny thing is that this home can keep getting bigger. When we open our hearts to more and more people and they move on in, our home expands. Then, if we let the trees and animals and other creatures in and start seeing them as part of our family too, things get really out of control, and we end up with the biggest home in the world.

In our naivete, we kids kept asking at each move, "Are we there yet?" hoping against hope that the answer would be yes.

And that's when we discover that no matter where we go, we've arrived. We're always home.

Dead Ants

*Why do you notice the splinter in your
    sister's eye,
but do not perceive the wooden beam
    in your own?*

Jesus (with slight adaptation!)

I have a high tolerance for messes, I'll admit. There's an upside and a downside to my tolerance, which is really a parental survival mechanism. The upside is that when I walk into my family room, I don't really *see* the mess anymore, and so I don't immediately scream and leave on the next bus out of town. The downside is that, well, messes stay longer than they "should."

But things really got out of hand last spring.

One night, after a particularly exhausting day, I put on my flannel nightgown, pulled back my bedsheet, and was about to drop into bed when I saw an ant. On my sheet. Heading toward my pillow. Knowing that one ant does not necessarily an army make, I searched for another, knowing that two means trouble. Sure enough, there was another. And another. I shouted for my husband, who stuck his head out of the bathroom door.

"Whd dr uwnt?" he asked, his mouth filled with toothpaste.

"We've got ants in the bed!" I yelled.

"Wght jst uminit," he answered helpfully.

I started my search for the trail and was looking so intently I almost missed it. Next to the bed, going up the wall, were a zillion ants. They went, in perfect formation, up the wall to the ceiling, where they took a left turn, moved to the corner, took another left, then a right, then a left, then another left, and finally, five walls later, entered their targeted destination: our bedroom linen closet. My nose was permanently scrunched up in the "Yuk!" position as I gingerly opened the door. The ants were merrily scaling their way down three shelves to their midnight snack—a bottle of cherry-flavored liquid Children's Tylenol.

"Raid," I exclaimed, turning to my husband, who had joined me. "We need Raid."

Now I'm not crazy about killing insects—especially after taking my daughter to see the movie *A Bug's Life*—but there were just too many of them and only one of me, and they had crossed the line by crawling on my pillow. So, after dragging a chair into the room, I apologized to them and sprayed their trail. The ants froze in place, and soon all were dead.

Since it was so late, we decided to leave them there and clean up in the morning. Certain that the spray would poison us as well, I opened the windows and turned on the ceiling fan, and then, after ten thorough inspections of our sheets, I climbed into bed. The room felt like a morgue.

"Yuk!" I shouted into the night.

"Go to sleep!" my husband responded.

The next morning, I looked at all the ants still stopped in their tracks. "I've *got* to clean them off the wall," I told myself. Of course, just then I had to drive my kids to school, so I put it off until later. That night, after I had climbed into bed, I realized the ants were still there, frozen in place. "Damn," I sighed, but I stayed snuggled under the sheets.

What I'm about to report is not a little embarrassing. Not for just one day, not for just one week, not even for just one month—but for more than three months, those ants stayed glued to my wall. I'm not sure exactly what happened. Mostly, I think I stopped seeing.

Now this onset of blindness may have been aggravated by the fact that the walls themselves were not a pretty sight to begin with. When we bought the house five years ago, we hated the bedroom wallpaper and were going to take it down and paint the walls before moving in. But one thing led to another, and it just never got done.

Four years later, I finally took some action and started peeling the wallpaper off, only it was glued on *really* well, and it shredded and stuck and was a bigger job than I had expected it would be. So I stopped, leaving it partially peeled, intending to get to it the next weekend. Then the next. You know the story. Even the ants, when they went marching up our walls, had to weave in and out of the wrinkles and grooves in the wallpaper. Ultimately, I just grew blind to the whole mess.

But that is not the worst of it. One day, while visiting my sister, who has three young children, one lizard, two cats, and two rats, I went into her bedroom to get something and saw that her bed wasn't made, clothes were strewn around, and a few toys were on the floor.

How can she live like this? I thought.

Grateful that I was not like her, I returned home and went upstairs. As I walked into my own bedroom, the ants started laughing at me.

Oops. I had been caught with Judging Mind. The humongous beam in my own eye had done a good job of blocking my sister's splinter.

The humongous beam in my own eye had done a good job of blocking my sister's splinter.

I washed the ants off my walls right then. It took a few more weeks before the walls were stripped and had a fresh coat of paint, but at last it is done.

Now if I could just get around to cleaning up the family room . . . or at least to recycling my 1991 issues of *Better Homes and Gardens.*

All Shall Be Well

I should begin by telling you why I am sitting here wearing this fluorescent-orange plastic hard hat and matching vinyl vest. I like to put them on just to remind myself that I am a Professional Rescuer.

I'll tell you where I got this designer set, but first you should know that I am also a Professional Worrier. Since I believe that anything can go wrong at any moment, it's important for me to plan for every eventuality so that I'm not caught unprepared. In my head there's a cassette tape playing an endless loop of concerns. When my husband asks me what I'm thinking about, I might, at any given moment, answer, "global warming, our checkbook's imbalance, kids, health insurance, my writing deadline, thinning hair, earthquakes, college tuition, overdue library books, nuclear weapons, and the dirty carpet." If I turn and ask my husband what he's thinking, he'll say something profound like "What's for dinner?"

> In my head there's a cassette tape playing an endless loop of concerns.

You may notice that in my list of worries I've included earthquakes. This is not a totally irrational fear, since I live in California and not Kansas. (Although scientists have discovered the Humboldt Fault running right through that state, in case those of you living there think you're fault free.) As a native Californian, I have lived through a number of Pretty Big Ones but am still waiting for THE BIG ONE.

We thought the Loma Prieta Quake of 1989 was It, but it turned out to be just a dress rehearsal. Come to think of it, I handled that one quite well. I happened to take off a little early from work that day. I had picked up the three boys at day care, and we all arrived home about twenty minutes before the jolt. When the house started shaking, I yelled for the kids to come stand with me in the doorway of the kitchen. I was taller than they were in those days, and I stood protectively over them, the four of us squeezing into the doorway.

"It's okay, guys, Mother Earth just needs to stretch," I said reassuringly. I was surprised at how calm I was. As it was happening, I didn't fear death as much as I feared that our newly painted walls would crack. The week before, my husband had kindly applied the sixth coat of paint to all the interior walls (the first two colors we tried were just a shade off). But the paint held up okay; the worst that happened was that the iron fell off the ironing board, a mirror broke, and the refrigerator died from a power surge that came when our electricity was restored three days later. The best that happened was that we met all our neighbors, ate picnic dinners on the front lawn, and discovered that unchangeable schedules could be changed.

Since then, however, I do feel a bit jumpy whenever I hear a loud noise or rumble. When large trucks drive by, I think they are tectonic plates shifting, and my body does its fight-or-flight routine. Adrenaline courses through my veins, and

I'm all ready, but with nowhere to go. When a minor temblor does hit, I lie awake at night doing word problems: If there are six people in the house, and each person should be allotted five gallons of water per day for a minimum three-day period, how many more gallons do we need if we already have a forty-gallon water tank that we could tap in an emergency? What if there are only four people, because two are away at college, and what if we need water for five days instead of three?

Then there are the storage questions: Where do we keep all this water? Do we keep it in the garage, which will be smashed into a pancake by our bedroom in a big quake and which we can't walk into on a good day because of the boys' weight machine, the boxes for Goodwill, numerous abandoned ceramic molds and jugs of liquid clay, and dozens of old college textbooks? Or do we put fifty-nine one-gallon jugs of water in the living room and try to camou-flage them by winding boughs of evergreen through their plastic handles in a Martha Stewartesque way, hoping nobody figures out what they really are?

This is why I lose sleep at night.

Back to the story behind my plastic hard hat and vest. It all began when I confessed to my sister that I lose sleep worrying about whether or not the Nutri-Grain bars I keep as an emergency food supply are still okay to eat. (I'm referring to the ones that I keep stored in a deteriorating Rubbermaid tub in the backyard so that the house will not fall on it during an earthquake.) Upon hearing this, my sister told me to get a grip. She said, "Maybe you should go see a therapist about all this." I said, "I *am* a therapist." She said, "So if you came in as a client to yourself, what would you tell you?" I pondered that one for a moment. "I would tell me, 'I know *just* how you feel!'"

I did get her point. It was time to do something about these worries of mine. As if by magic, a brochure from city hall arrived announcing a home emergency training program. In this class, firefighters teach residents how to handle earthquakes and other major disasters. Remembering the proverb "Trust in Allah, but tie up your camel," I knew that this class was the answer to my prayers. "Trust in God, but take the class." I signed up immediately.

The nice thing about taking such training courses is that you get to meet other neurotic people like yourself. Not that I don't meet neurotic people in other places—as a therapist, I tend to hang out with such folks during my working hours. But these classmates shared *my* neurosis, and it was strangely comforting. It's rare that I run into people who are willing to discuss what type of wrench is best for shutting off the gas.

For six weeks, we learned about all kinds of emergencies and how to handle them. It was wonderful. But the best part was on the final evening, when we got to put all this learning into practice. The firefighters presented us with our orange plastic safety hats and vests, and we knew we had arrived! We were now members of the Home Emergency Assistance Team (otherwise known as H.E.A.T.).

Donning my hard hat and vest, I extinguished fires, performed a search and rescue operation, triaged victims who were trapped under rubble, climbed tall buildings with a single bound. I even lifted a VW Bug (which looked suspiciously like an old boyfriend's) off of a dummy (which looked suspiciously like the old boyfriend) by using a long plank of wood as a lever.

Then I knew how Superman must feel in his cape. What strength! What power! This is why I occasionally like to take out my hard hat and put it on. Even though it's made of plastic and the inside tag warns that it only protects against small falling objects, it makes me look like a Professional Rescuer. It makes me feel like a Professional Rescuer.

My kids think it makes me look silly.

After I finished the class and was just beginning to believe that it might be safe to get a good night's sleep, I read a captivating article in *Discover* magazine: "Twenty Ways the World Could End Suddenly." Here were scenarios beyond my wildest imaginings. Asteroid impacts that could wipe out all life, including cockroaches (which might not be such a bad thing). Rogue black holes that sneak up and swallow the earth whole. Giant solar flares that fry the planets. A reversal of the earth's magnetic field, which could send us all out of orbit. Mass insanity. Robots taking over.

I had a sinking feeling that being a member of H.E.A.T. was not going to help me out very much in these scenarios.

But as I read and realized how many gigantic things could go wrong, I actually calmed down. Such incredible events are so out of my control that even *my* ego can't pretend that it can do anything to deter them. My perspective shifted, and suddenly earthquakes seemed to be relatively minor events.

The fact of the matter is that the universe is huge and ancient, and it's going to do what it's going to do. If I go through life thinking it's me versus the universe, I lose every time. But if I realize it's me *in* the universe, I relax. I'm part of this extraordinary, terrifying, amazing creation, and I'll experience all that goes with it: the good stuff, the scary stuff, the big bumps, and the little bumps. The Serenity Prayer takes on even more meaning when I look at life from this cosmic angle: God grant me the serenity to accept the things I cannot change, courage to change the things I can, and wisdom to know the difference. A rogue black hole is simply one of those things I cannot change, and I know for a fact that my orange vest won't fend off solar flares.

And so now I'm taking off my hard hat and vest and putting them away in an old box marked "Xerox 4024DP Copy Paper." This is my emergency supply kit. It is where I keep the hat and vest, along with a package of disposable diapers (to use as bandages), three plastic garbage bags, first aid supplies, and the training manual that reminds me of what I'm supposed to do.

Where to store this box is an issue. I used to keep it on top of my clothes dryer, but then I realized that that was a foolish idea because it is a gas dryer, and the cleaning supplies that are stored in the cupboard above it could fall onto the floor and be ignited by the pilot light, setting the kit on fire. I tried to solve this problem by attaching a plastic latch onto the cupboard door handles, but the boys keep forgetting to replace the latch after they use the Comet (which, now that I think about it, is not very frequently). But since being a member of H.E.A.T. means that I am supposed to lead any neighborhood volunteer rescue effort and, as the leader, keep my emergency kit with me during all operations, I thought I should move it to a safer location.

So now this box sits in the entryway between the front door and the kitchen. I've placed a nice silk plant on top of it, but I don't think anyone has been fooled into thinking it's a table. It does blend fairly well with the rest of our decor: Early Mess. Nobody would guess that The Plan To Save the Neighborhood is hidden in this little box. Whenever I pass it, I'm reminded of the proverb "Trust in God, and be a H.E.A.T. member."

At least I've accomplished half of that equation. Now I'm working on the other half. I know that one of my major life tasks revolves around developing trust. I remind myself of the comforting message that Julian of Norwich, a mystic in the fourteenth century, received in her prayer: "All shall be well, and all shall be well, and all manner of things shall be well." This is a nice antidote for my obsessions about earthquakes and robots taking over, and it helps me to remember that whatever happens, somebody bigger than me is in charge.

Thank goodness. Because while I enjoy wearing my hard hat and vest, the extent to which they'll help me is pretty limited. And while I don't know that I'll ever be fully over my fears, I do know that any progress I can make in the Trust Department will be of immense help to the world. After all, I wouldn't want my anxieties to increase the likelihood of mass insanity.

All shall be well.

Transfiguration

But our time together was so short, like the swim in the lake, it would be gone in a blink, and I wondered how I could possibly hold on to this moment . . . I wanted time to stop, so I could be there forever with them, with the children I had made.

Lenore P. (quoted in *Writing from Life*)

There are times—moments—when life shines a spotlight down upon you, illuminating that moment as a holy moment . . .

A moment when you live half in and half out of time, when you know utterly and completely that *this* is a wonderful moment. And you know equally well that it is fleeting and will pass.

A moment when the music is so magnificent that your heart fills to the point of breaking open, when a note hangs in the air and all eternity is, just for that moment, made manifest.

A moment that is so achingly beautiful that even though you know time moves forward, your heart pleads for a time-out so that you can hold on to this moment and place and sense of absolute wholeness.

That last Friday in August was one of those moments in my life.

Unbelievably, eighteen years had slipped by, and my oldest child, Benjamin, was leaving the next week for college. Like the proverbial mother hen, I gathered my four children, three of them towering over me, and set out to have one last picnic with them. We drove to Shoreline Park, a beautiful marina near San Francisco Bay where sailboats and windsails are launched, released to dance on the water. The brilliant blues of the bay and the sky, along with the abundant greens of the grasses and trees, created a backdrop for the symphony of sounds made up of people's laughter and of the distinct calls of seagulls and Canada geese. We spread out a colorful Mexican blanket on a rolling hill, and the boys set down the cooler and picked up their football. Soon they were tackling, tickling, teasing, and taunting one another, gently including their little sister whenever she was able to catch up, breathless with excitement.

As I watched my beautiful boys, I thought back to a day some ten years ago. They were little ones then—ages four, six, and eight—and we were sitting and eating ice-cream cones at an outdoor restaurant. Another family walked by, and they too had three boys, but these were teenagers, and they were almost a foot taller than their parents. I felt at that moment as if I were getting a peek into the future—one day my boys would be fourteen, sixteen, and eighteen, and they would tower over me. Well, that day was here, and I never wanted it to end.

Through the years, I have heard again and again that we should cherish the time we have with our children, that before we know it they will be grown and gone. Often I freeze-frame moments, creating memories that I hope will be forever etched in my mind. But even those things that I thought I would never forget—the first word, the newborn smell, the favorite toy—fade more quickly than I ever believed possible. And now, as I sat in the last remaining moments of our time as a family with four "kids," I knew that there was no going back. Like the times just before I gave birth, I realized there was no stopping this process of launching children.

We learn, along with Peter, that as much as we'd like to stay up on mountain-tops, we have to come back to earth.

I remembered one of the truths that the Buddha taught about life experience—that of *anicca,* or impermanence, the constantly changing nature of all things. That concept is found in the Christian Scriptures as well. One example is the story in which Jesus brings Peter, James, and John with him up the mountain to pray. While they are all up there, Jesus' clothes become a dazzling white; then Elijah and Moses come to chat with him. Peter wants to make tents for the three of them, in the hope that this can become a permanent arrangement. But Jesus nixes that idea, and after the two ancestors disappear, he leads the disciples back down to sea level. We learn, along with Peter, that as much as we'd like to stay up on mountaintops, we have to come back to earth. We have to keep moving, for life keeps changing.

I'll be honest. If given the chance, I would've liked to put up some tents right there at the Shoreline Boat Launch and Park. But the boys preferred the sailboats. With my heart aching from joy and from sadness, I realized that summer was over. I sat looking at my children, took a long, deep breath, and smiled.

Blankies

I'm finding threads of love all around me.

Julianna's blanket is unraveling. It started its life as a beautiful weave of pastel pinks and yellows and blues. But now the slender threads are breaking off, and we're finding them in the car, on the stairs, under the church pew. She tries to collect them one by one and has even attempted to tape them back onto what's left of her blanket. But several years of snuggles are taking their toll.

I am reluctant to put her blankie through the ordeal of washing and drying it. With each wash the holes become larger, the threads fewer. When it becomes imperative to clean it, I wait until she's at school. She always knows it has been cleaned; when she holds it to her face and breathes deeply, her scent is no longer captured in its threads.

This blankie has helped her to feel some sense of security in a sometimes scary world. It is her portable anchor; with it, she can soothe herself in almost any situation. We have driven across town to retrieve it; we have searched for hours when it's been misplaced. One day, I accidentally dropped it in the library parking lot. When we realized it was missing an hour later, I retraced my steps and returned to the library. As I drove up, I smiled. The blankie was

spread out over a bush like a signal flag. I knew someone
had recognized its blankieness and had set it carefully in
plain view for its worried owner.

It is not only little ones who find blankies or other "lovies"
comforting. A friend of ours has a twelve-year-old son who
slings around what is left of a white stuffed dog. It has no
eyes, no mouth, no hair, and some gaping wounds. Yet it
still does its job. Another friend has a thirteen-year-old
daughter whose blankie was originally two feet by three feet
and now is only one foot square. Every morning she holds
it to her face and takes a long deep breath before going out
to brave junior high.

Each of my sons has loved a blankie. Ben owned two, but
truly cherished only one. His grandmother made him a
beautifully quilted yellow blanket, and I made him a red
patchwork one. I was a new mother and a newer seamstress.
The fabric I selected was too light in weight, and the dozens
of red yarn ties, which I had carefully placed at the corner
of each little square, tore holes in the material. I did not
know how to make the stitching solid, and after several
washings, all the batting clumped in one corner. I took it
out of the dryer and cried.

His grandmother's blanket was, and is, Ben's favorite. When
he went away to college, he left it behind on his bed—I
suspect as a place marker, a reminder to him, and to us,
that he can always come home.

And his red blanket? It is folded away in a box in the
garage. It is waiting to be mended; it has been waiting for

almost two decades. Occasionally Ben reminds me that I promised to repair its holes. I'm not sure why I delay. Perhaps it symbolizes for me my inexpert beginnings as a mother. Perhaps it is my way of holding on, by leaving one thing undone.

When David was born nineteen months after Ben, I had learned from some of my mistakes. I made him a blanket out of strong blue flannel. His grandmother made him a blanket as well, but I do not remember what it looks like. David chose mine. It still looks like new, mostly because David never dragged it around with him. He always left it on his bed, even when he was a toddler.

When David left for college, I watched with surprise as my son, who could hardly wait to be off to his independent life, packed this blanket in his suitcase. This, it turned out, was not so unusual. In the dorm elevator, we saw numerous stuffed animals and blankies being moved into their owners' new homes.

Once in his dorm room, David spread his blue blanket on top of his khaki comforter. When he left the room, I found myself tucking it away under the comforter, afraid that his roommate might not understand. David came back in, saw his blanket poking out from under his bedspread, and shook his head with a smile. We both realized it was no longer my job to protect him. He gave me a long hug good-bye.

Matt was born thirty months after David; with three boys under the age of four, I did not have the time or energy to sew another blanket. Once again, his grandmother outdid herself, embroidering an elaborate alphabet on one side of a red-and-white quilted blanket. Matthew named it "Reddy" and loved it to pieces. Eventually I had to cut away the shreds of embroidery and reconstruct the blanket into a slightly smaller version.

Most of the time Reddy is under its fifteen-year-old owner's bed or hidden somewhere else in his messy room. Nowadays Matt wraps himself in a full-size red-and-white comforter that he pulls off his bed, looking like royalty as he wanders down to sit at the computer. Sometimes I complain about how he drags it over dusty floors, but not often. I know that all too soon Matt, Reddy, and the comforter will be leaving home.

When I was pregnant with Julianna, I wanted to make her a blanket, but time slipped away. One friend gave Julianna the beautifully woven blanket that she loves, and another couple gave her a small quilt that their daughter had outgrown. These are known as Big Blankie and Little Blankie. Big usually stays on her bed; Little is her constant companion.

And now Little Blankie is falling apart. And so, with years of experience behind me, I take out my sewing machine and make an attempt to salvage the blanket. It cannot be rewoven, and so I take a large square of plain white cotton and ask Julianna to place what's left of her beloved woven threads into the center. Then I fold the fabric in half, wrapping the essence of blankie inside. I stitch all along the outside, careful to leave some of the pastel threads peeking through the stitching.

When I am done, there is a long pause as she picks it up. Wide-eyed, she looks at her precious parcel, and I hold my breath.

"Look, I can see the threads! Thank you, Mama." She climbs onto my lap. We are both relieved.

We sit there for a long time and snuggle. At this point in my life, even a single thread of love provides all the comfort I need. I wrap myself in my memories and in the joy of present moments, resting in a warm and anchored place as I hold my children close and as I learn to let them go.

EPILOGUE: A BLESSING FOR YOUR JOURNEY

This part of our journey together now draws to an end. The work we are doing each day is so important, and it makes all the difference to know that we are doing it together. We do our meditations, our prayers, our simple activities of love not just for ourselves, but for all of us.

Julianna reminded me of this profound connection we have to one another. On our way to school last week, she sat in her car seat, looking thoughtfully out of the van window. Then she called out my name.

"Mama," she said.

"What, sweetie?" I asked.

"The whole world is inside of you."

I looked in the rearview mirror at her smiling face. "The whole world is inside of you," she repeated. "And inside of me."

When we look deeply and love graciously, we engage in a spiritual practice that transforms not only us, but our entire world.

I offer you a blessing until we meet again.

> May you discover the Sacred in the center of your world,
> and may you welcome moments of grace.
>
> May your eyes find signs along your path,
> and your ears hear the holiness that surrounds you.
> May your life be blessed with good companions,
> and may your heart grow in wisdom and compassion.
>
> May you teach your children to sing and to dance,
> and to know the sheer joy of celebration.
> May you tell stories to one another all of your days,
> and may you grow to love the sweet comfort of silence.
>
> May you care for the earth as your home,
> and may passion give life to your work.
> May what you do be for the benefit of all,
> and may your love extend to all generations.
>
> May the blessings of love be always upon you,
> and may all the dreams on your journey be fulfilled.

APPENDIX

Many people have asked me for a list of the questions that I mention in the story "The Mother of Men." I include it here. Usually the men let the thirteen-year-old choose which questions to discuss, and often they end up only addressing two or three of these questions on any one weekend. They also add other questions along the way.

Also, I might add that soon the women in our families will hold a blessing ritual for one of our girls, who will be entering puberty. We will gather to celebrate and to welcome her into the circle of women.

ON BEING/BECOMING A MAN

Who are my heroes?

What is my philosophy of life?

What do I feel about work?

What gives meaning to my life?

What are the qualities of my mother I admire? Of my father?

What qualities do I value in a relationship?

What does intimacy mean?

What are my dreams for myself?

What does success mean to me?

What brings me joy?

For what, or whom, would I sacrifice my time, my energy, my health, my life?

What is my idea of power? What is the source of my power?

What are my gifts?

What do I fear?

What is sacred?

Who are my people?

How do I most enjoy life?

NOTES

I. DRIVING LESSONS

p. 3, Jon Kabat-Zinn, *Wherever You Go, There You Are: Mindfulness Meditation in Everyday Life* (New York: Hyperion, 1994).

p. 4, Frederick Buechner, *The Eyes of the Heart: A Memoir of the Lost and Found* (San Francisco: HarperSanFrancisco, 1999), 97.

"CHEESE LADY"

p. 5, Thomas Merton, *New Seeds of Contemplation* (New York: New Directions, 1961), 98.

"CARMA"

p. 9, Margaret L. Mitchell, untitled poem, *Ms. Magazine*, December 1987, 44.

p. 15, Gary Snyder, quoted in Jack Kornfield, *After the Ecstasy, the Laundry: How the Heart Grows Wise on the Spiritual Path* (New York: Bantam, 2000), 228–29.

"I'M NOT NICE ANYMORE"

p. 16, Fay Weldon, quoted in Harriet Lerner, *The Mother Dance: How Children Change Your Life* (New York: HarperCollins, 1998), 242.

p. 17, Anne Lamott, *Word by Word,* (Austin, Tex.: Writer's AudioShop, 1996), audiocassette.

pp. 17–18, Harriet Lerner, *The Mother Dance,* 309.

p. 18, Linda Eyre, *I Didn't Plan to Be a Witch: And Other Surprises of a Joyful Mother* (New York: Simon & Schuster, 1996).

" T E E N S "
p. 23, Patt and Steve Saso, *10 Best Gifts for Your Teen: Raising Teens with Love and Understanding* (Notre Dame, Ind.: Sorin, 1999).

" K I T C H E N   W I S D O M "
p. 28, Rachel Naomi Remen, *Kitchen Table Wisdom: Stories That Heal* (New York: Riverhead, 1996).

p. 32, Mary Roach, "Family Matters," *San Francisco,* December 1998, 65.

p. 34, Rachel Naomi Remen, *My Grandfather's Blessings: Stories of Strength, Refuge, and Belonging* (New York: Riverhead, 2000), 216.

I I .   B R E A T H I N G   L E S S O N S
p. 45, Thich Nhat Hanh, *Peace Is Every Step: The Path of Mindfulness in Everyday Life* (New York: Bantam Books, 1991), 8.

" S I T T I N G   I N   H A P P Y "
p. 48, Vimala McClure, *The Tao of Motherhood* (Novato, Calif.: New World Library, 1997), 103.

p. 49, Thich Nhat Hanh, *Peace Is Every Step,* 10.

p. 50, Psalm 131 quoted from The New American Bible.

" D O O R S "

p. 51, Bamidbar Rabba 12:4, cited in Lawrence Kushner, *Eyes Remade for Wonder: A Lawrence Kushner Reader* (Woodstock, Vt.: Jewish Lights, 1998), 17.

" T H R E E   M O M E N T S   O F   G R A C E "

p. 54, Frederick Buechner, *The Magnificent Defeat* (New York: Seabury, 1968), 87.

p. 55, The story about blessings that are not packaged in ways we expect appears on numerous Web sites. The author is unknown.

pp. 57–58, Rachel Naomi Remen, *Kitchen Table Wisdom*, 214.

p. 58, Kathleen Norris, *Amazing Grace: A Vocabulary of Faith* (New York: Riverhead, 1998), 150–51.

" T E L E P H O N E   M E D I T A T I O N ,
T A K E   2 "

pp. 72–73, 75, Thich Nhat Hanh, *Peace Is Every Step*, 29–31.

I I I .   M U S I C   L E S S O N S

p. 79, Swami Kripalvanandji (called "Bapuji" by his disciples), "Music and the Search for God," available online at http://www.spiritsound.com/bapuji.html.

p. 81, Angeles Arrien, quoted in Natalie Rogers, *The Creative Connection: Expressive Arts As Healing* (Palo Alto, Calif.: Science and Behavior Books, 1993), 48.

" I N V I S I B L E   F R I E N D S "
p. 94, Jelaluddin Rumi, *The Essential Rumi*, trans. Coleman Barks, with John Moyne, A. J. Arberry, and Reynold Nicholson (San Francisco: Harper, 1995), 169–70.

" B E D T I M E   B L E S S I N G S "
p. 98, Robert Fulghum, *From Beginning to End: The Rituals of Our Lives* (New York: Villard, 1995), 53.

" P O T A T O   S T O R I E S "
p. 102, Susan Wittig Albert, *Writing from Life: Telling Your Soul's Story* (New York: Putnam, 1997), 172.

pp. 104–105, The story about a sack of potatoes and forgiveness appears on numerous Web sites. The author is unknown.

pp. 106–107, Leigh Brasington, "Mental Proliferation," available online at http://www.geocities.com/Tokyo/6774/papanca.htm.

I V .   E A R T H   L E S S O N S
p. 120, Pierre Teilhard de Chardin, *Hymn of the Universe* (New York: Harper & Row, 1965), 28.

p. 120, John G. Neihardt, et al. *Black Elk Speaks: Being the Life Story of a Holy Man of the Oglala Sioux as told through John G. Neihardt (Flaming Rainbow)* (Lincoln: University of Nebraska Press, 1979).

p. 120, Victor Perera and Robert D. Bruce, *The Last Lords of Palenque: The Lacandón Mayas of the Mexican Rain Forest* (Boston: Little Brown, 1982).

" N I G H T "

p. 126, Jane Ellen Mauldin, *Glory, Hallelujah! Now Please Pick up Your Socks* (Boston: Skinner House, 1998), 11–12.

" B L E S S I N G   O N E   A N O T H E R "

p. 136, Galway Kinnell, "Saint Francis and the Sow," in *Three Books: Body Rags; Mortal Acts, Mortal Words; The Past* (Boston: Houghton Mifflin, 1993).

" T H E   W I S D O M   O F   T H E   H E A R T "

p. 142, Rachel Naomi Remen, *Kitchen Table Wisdom,* 140.

" T H E   M O T H E R ' S   J O U R N E Y "

p. 150, Zelma Brown, "Nurtured," from the multimedia show, *MY SISTER, MY SISTER.* Information is available online at: www.sistersproject.org.

" H O L Y   G R O U N D "

p. 159, Annie Dillard, *Pilgrim at Tinker Creek* (New York: HarperPerennial, 1998), 200–201.

" A L L   S H A L L   B E   W E L L "

p. 189, Corey S. Powell, "Twenty Ways the World Could End Suddenly," *Discover,* October 2000, 50.

" T R A N S F I G U R A T I O N "

p. 193, Lenore P., quoted in Susan Wittig Albert, *Writing from Life,* 113.

PERMISSIONS

CONTACT THE AUTHOR

Information on workshops and seminars offered by Denise Roy can be found on her Web site, www.familyspirit.com, where you can also sign up to receive her free online newsletter.

You can reach her by mail c/o Trade Editorial Department, Loyola Press, 3441 N. Ashland Avenue, Chicago, IL, 60657, or by e-mail at denise@familyspirit.com. She would love to hear from you.

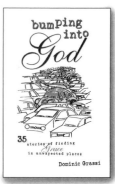